THE
AFFIRMATIVE ACTION
HANDBOOK

THE AFFIRMATIVE ACTION HANDBOOK

Dealing With Day-to-Day Supervisory Problems

by Stephen Sahlein

Edited by Jeff Baron

Executive Enterprises Publications Co., Inc.
33 West 60th Street, New York, New York 10023

STEPHEN SAHLEIN writes on business, management, and finance for various publications. He has created and written a number of business newsletters including *The EEO Review*.

JEFF BARON has an M.B.A. from Harvard Business School. He has done extensive writing and consulting on the subject of equal employment opportunity.

Second Printing, 1979

ISBN 0-917386-21-3

© 1978 Executive Enterprises Publications Co., Inc., New York. All rights reserved, including the right to reproduce this book or portions thereof, in any form, except for the inclusion of brief quotations in a review. All inquiries should be addressed to Executive Enterprises Publications Co., Inc., 33 West 60th Street, New York, New York 10023.

Printed in the United States of America by Ganis and Harris, New York.

CONTENTS

INTRODUCTION

PART ONE 3

    Hiring Practices   4
    Evaluation Practices   21
    Promotion Practices   29
    Discipline Practices   36
    Employees Filing Charges   44

PART TWO 53

    Sex Discrimination   54
    Race and National Origin Discrimination   65
    Religious Discrimination   76
    Age Discrimination   82
    Discrimination Against the Handicapped   85
    Reverse Discrimination   91

PART THREE 99

    Federal Laws Against Discrimination   100
    Part-Time and Temporary Employees   103
    Glossary of EEO Terms   107

Introduction

It would take a lawyer, and a brilliant lawyer at that, to look at a law and interpret it for every possible situation to which it might apply. Yet every supervisor, whether office manager, plant foreman, or corporation president, is held responsible by the government for obeying Equal Employment Opportunity (EEO) laws, in all their complexity.

Many companies have learned about their EEO responsibility the hard way. Discrimination suits have brought some very costly settlements. It is crucial to understand the way EEO laws apply to you and your company, to identify possible violations, and to change those policies in order to eliminate job discrimination.

The Affirmative Action Handbook takes those complex laws, discusses them in simple terms, and breaks them down by application. If you're about to conduct an employment interview, the section on hiring will tell you what you can and can't ask. If your older employees are grumbling, the section on age discrimination will help you see why, and more important, help you prevent that grumbling from turning into a lawsuit.

The points made in each section are brought home by actual case studies. These will help you translate the ideas to experiences that you may have had, and help you avoid some of the problems you'll read about.

Much of the material in this book has appeared in *EEO Review,* a monthly newsletter published by Executive Enterprises Publications Co., Inc. The material has been organized here in such a way as to make *The Affirmative Action Handbook* a powerful working document, a book you'll want to refer to often.

Part One

Equal employment opportunity is one of a supervisor's many daily concerns. There are certain times when a supervisor's EEO responsibility comes out of the background into the spotlight. These are the areas where discrimination has traditionally been a roadblock for certain groups.

The following section examines the supervisor's role in hiring, evaluating, promoting, and disciplining employees. It includes basic guidelines for avoiding discrimination and case studies which illustrate these points. It concludes with a look at the problem of supervising employees who have filed discrimination charges.

HIRING PRACTICES

Many employers are not hiring the best people for the job. Some highly qualified people never get a chance to prove themselves, because of discrimination in the hiring process. Aside from being bad business, discriminatory hiring practices are more and more frequently the target of lawsuits.

One cause of job segregation—that situation in which blacks, women, etc. end up in only one kind of job or are kept out of another—can be the job description. That's because if the description is out-of-date or contains misleading language it may attract certain groups while turning away others. You can make an important contribution to your organization's EEO efforts by periodically reviewing the job descriptions in your department to correct inaccuracies, to eliminate old and unnecessary job qualifications, add new ones, and clean up any excess verbiage that, at best, is gathering dust and, at worst, is deterring qualified applicants from applying for the job.

Questions you should be asking in reviewing job descriptions include:

• **Are the functions described in the job description still a part of the actual job?** If not, eliminate them. For example, in factory work, some parts of the job may not be automated, and, in office work, certain clerical tasks may have been computerized.

• **Is every part of the job included in the job description?** If jobs have been merged, or new responsibilities added, make sure they're included in the written description. When minority, female, Spanish-surnamed, handicapped, or older applicants apply for an opening and find out there is a part of the job that was not listed in the description they saw, they may suspect that these requirements were added after they applied to discourage them. Even worse, if they actually get the job and

Dealing with Day-to-Day Supervisory Problems

are expected to perform some function they didn't know about—and possibly can't do—they may think these functions were added so that you or the company would have an excuse for firing them.

• **Does the job description demand greater technical knowledge than is actually needed to do the work?** For example, you don't need to know anything about electronics to package radios or to assemble desk lamps.

• **If specific technical background or training is required, is the extent of that background or training accurately reflected in the job description?** Watch out for educational overkill in job requirements. Does the applicant really need a degree in an area or would completion of a single course be enough?

• **Do the employees currently doing the job have the skills or education listed in the job description?** If they don't, see if these requirements might be removed. Technology may have made some jobs more complex, but it has made many jobs simpler. More importantly, expertise can be gained outside of school or without special training. For example, there are people who can diagnose car problems and repair them as well, even though they've never had any actual training in that area. They simply learned how to do it through a combination of talent, interest, and personal drive. To put it another way, if *knowledge,* rather than education or training, is required, see if you can have the job description changed to reflect this: "Knowledge of (rather than "training in") mechanics required."

• **Does the job description describe the work in elevated language that distorts the actual nature of the job?** This is sometimes done to make the job appear to be more glamorous than it really is, either to attract applicants or to give them the idea that the job has "prestige." However, an indirect result of this verbal inflation may be to deter qualified minority or female applicants who have limited education and who are intimidated by high-sounding language. In the following example, a regular secretarial job, consisting of routine secretarial tasks, was listed in a newspaper under the title "Editorial Trainee," and read:

> *Handle broad contact with authors, rewrite, edit, some research. Work under deadline pressure. Typing, shorthand required.*

But when this description is deflated or "translated" into its components, the actual day-to-day chores, it turns out the applicant doesn't need to know anything about editing:

Job Description	Actual Job
Editorial Trainee	*Secretary*
"broad contact with authors"	Talking to authors on the phone simply to give or take messages; set-up or verify appointments; typing letters to authors, filing correspondence from them.
"rewrite"	Compose a business letter out of someone's scribbled message.
"edit"	Catch boss's typos, mispellings, etc.
"research"	Check addresses or company/client names in phone directory.
"work under deadline pressure"	Simply means getting letters out, collating manuscripts, etc. by a certain time. The deadline pressure is there, but the "trainee's" part in it is strictly secretarial.
"typing, shorthand required"	The heart of the job; what the individual will spend 99% of the time doing.

There are many minority job-seekers (or employees seeking upgrading or transfer within an organization) who could do this job, but who might feel inadequate in the face of this fancy language. The result might be that the job is consistently occupied by white, rather than black, Chicano or Spanish-surnamed employees. Or else high turnover caused by hiring overqualified people who fit the job description rather than the job.

Dealing with Day-to-Day Supervisory Problems

Another way to check on job descriptions indirectly is to look at the people doing the jobs. Is one kind of work done by all white males? All blacks? All women? If it is, look at the job description to see if the requirements tend to screen out minorities or women, or, on the other hand, to suggest that blacks rather than whites fill the job. Are there unlawful requirements that might affect certain groups such as height or ability to lift heavy weight where neither is really needed to perform the work?

Once you know what you need, you're ready to determine the best person to fill that need. In advertising or posting a job, use the above guidelines for describing the job.

Reviewing and deciding among applicants is a difficult task. The process is made more complicated, yet ultimately more equitable and more effective by the requirements of EEO regulations.

The following is a simple guide by subject area to what you can ask applicants. These apply both to the employment application and the interview. It should help you isolate what you *need* to know from a job applicant, as opposed to what you'd *like* to know or are used to asking. At the same time, it will help you avoid common discriminatory pitfalls.

Subject Area	EEO Do's and Don't's for Interviewing Job Applicants
Age	ACCEPTABLE PRE-EMPLOYMENT INQUIRIES: None. (The exception, as always, is when you can prove that age is a *bona fide occupational qualification*—i.e., is necessary to perform the job; usually difficult or impossible to prove.) NOTE: A pre-employment application may request the applicant's age or date of birth. The Labor Department recommends also including a disclaimer to the effect that age will not be used in any employment decision in accordance with the Age Discrimination Act.

Subject Area	EEO Do's and Don't's for Interviewing Job Applicants
	INADVISABLE PRE-EMPLOYMENT INQUIRIES: Any question designed to discover someone's age.
Arrest Record	ACCEPTABLE: None. (Law enforcement agencies are exempt from this restriction, but should call their local EEOC office to see what the exceptions are.) INADVISABLE: Any inquiry relating to arrests. Since, under our judicial system, you are presumed innocent until *proven* guilty—i.e., convicted—records of arrests without conviction are meaningless.
Availability for Saturday or Sunday work (pertaining to religious discrimination)	ACCEPTABLE: Although you may want to know about an applicant's availability for Saturday or Sunday work, the answer may not do you any good since even when an applicant's religious observance makes him or her unavailable for weekend shifts, this fact cannot be used in any hiring decision. Title VII requires employers to make "reasonable accommodation" even for "a *prospective employee's* [emphasis added] religious observance", unless it causes "undue hardship." If you decide to ask, let the applicant know that a reasonable effort will be made to accommodate any religious needs should he or she be hired. INADVISABLE: Any question about religious observance.

Dealing with Day-to-Day Supervisory Problems

Subject Area	EEO Do's and Don't's for Interviewing Job Applicants
Availability for weekend or evening work (pertaining to sex discrimination).	ACCEPTABLE: Inquiries about an applicant's availability for evening and/or weekend work *provided that* the inquiry is made of both male and female applicants and *provided that* the person now doing the job works evenings and/or weekends, or that a definite change in schedule is being implemented. INADVISABLE: Asking this question because you *think* you'll want the person to work evenings or weekends. (Reason: Question is likely to have an excessive and therefore discriminatory impact on applicants with families—particularly women.)
Citizenship	ACCEPTABLE: Whether the applicant is prevented from lawfully becoming employed in this country because of visa or immigration status. Whether applicant can provide proof of citizenship, visa, alien registration number after being hired. INADVISABLE: Whether applicant is a citizen. Any requirement that the applicant present birth, naturalization, or baptismal certificate before being hired.
Convictions	ACCEPTABLE: It is all right to inquire about an applicant's conviction record for "security sensitive" jobs, since it has been shown that people with high conviction rates are poor risks for these jobs. "Security sensitive" jobs include not only the obvious—treasurer, cashier, etc.—but peripheral positions as

Subject Area	EEO Do's and Don't's for Interviewing Job Applicants
	well—janitor, typist, trucker or other jobs where the employee would be working in or near a security sensitive area. (Check your state and local laws, some of which are more restrictive.) INADVISABLE: Questions about conviction unrelated to job requirements—e.g., inquiries about gambling arrests for the job of pipefitter.
Credit inquiries	ACCEPTABLE: None, unless job related. INADVISABLE: Inquiries about charge accounts, bank accounts, etc.
Education	ACCEPTABLE: If the individual has the specific education or training required for the specific job. INADVISABLE: General questions about high school or college degrees unless you (or your supervisors) can *prove* the educational degree inquired about is necessary to perform the job.
Family status	ACCEPTABLE: Whether applicant has any activities, commitments, or responsibilities that might prevent him or her from meeting work schedules or attendance requirements. NOTE: These questions *must* be asked of both men and women or of neither. It is unlawful to ask this only of women or only of men. INADVISABLE: Whether the applicant is married or single, number and age of children, spouse's job, spouse's or applicant's

Dealing with Day-to-Day Supervisory Problems 11

Subject Area	EEO Do's and Don't's for Interviewing Job Applicants
	family responsibilities. Any question asked only of one sex—e.g., asking only women about child-care arrangements.
Financial status	ACCEPTABLE: None. INADVISABLE: Inquiries about an applicant's financial condition. This has been found to result in discrimination against minorities since more non-whites than whites are below the poverty level. Questions about home ownership or car ownership (unless owning a car is required for the job).
Handicaps	ACCEPTABLE: Whether applicant has a specific mental or physical handicap which relates to fitness to perform the particular job. Whether applicant has handicaps which should be taken into account in deciding job placement. INADVISABLE: General inquiries—e.g., "Do you have any handicaps?"—which might reveal handicaps not related to fitness to perform specific job.
Height and Weight	ACCEPTABLE: Inquiries about ability to perform the job (without mentioning the person's height or weight). Protects those of Spanish, Asian background and women. INADVISABLE: Any inquiry about height or weight not based on the actual job requirements, in which case you or your superiors must be able to prove that a specific, mini-

Subject Area	EEO Do's and Don't's for Interviewing Job Applicants
	mum or maximum height or weight is required to perform the job.
Marital status	ACCEPTABLE: None. INADVISABLE: Whether the applicant is married, single, divorced, separated, engaged, widowed.
Military	ACCEPTABLE: Inquiries about education, training, or work experience gained in U.S. armed forces. INADVISABLE: Type or condition of military discharge. Experience in other than U.S. armed forces. Request for discharge papers.
National origin	ACCEPTABLE: Inquiries into applicant's ability to read, write and speak English or foreign languages when required for a specific job. INADVISABLE: Questions about applicant's lineage, ancestry, national origin, descent, place of birth, or mother tongue, national origin of applicant's parents or spouse. How applicant acquired ability to read, write or speak a foreign language.
Organization	ACCEPTABLE: Inquiries about membership in professional organizations related to the job—e.g., does the applicant for a chemical engineering job belong to a chemical engineering society. INADVISABLE: Questions about organizations whose name or character indicates

Dealing with Day-to-Day Supervisory Problems 13

Subject Area	EEO Do's and Don't's for Interviewing Job Applicants
	members' economic or social class, race, color, creed, sex, marital status, religion or national origin—e.g., country clubs, social clubs, religious clubs, fraternal orders.
Personal information	ACCEPTABLE: Whether the applicant has ever worked for your organization. Whether the applicant has ever worked for your organization under another name. Names of character references. INADVISABLE: General inquiries about change of name through application in court or marriage.
Pregnancy	ACCEPTABLE: Inquiries about the applicant's anticipated duration of stay on the job or anticipated absences—only if made to both male and female applicants. INADVISABLE: Any question relating to pregnancy or medical history concerning pregnancy. NOTE: the EEOC has rules that to refuse to hire a female solely because she is pregnant amounts to sex discrimination.
Race or color	ACCEPTABLE: None. INADVISABLE: Any questions about race or color.
Relatives	ACCEPTABLE: Name of applicant's relatives already employed by your organization or competitor. (This inquiry becomes *un*lawful when hiring preference is given to relatives of employees at a time when minorities are

Subject Area	EEO Do's and Don't's for Interviewing Job Applicants
	under-represented in your organization's work force.) INADVISABLE: Requests for the names and addresses of any relatives other than those working for your organization.
Religion or creed	ACCEPTABLE: None. INADVISABLE: Questions about applicant's religious denomination, religious affiliation, church, parish, pastor, or religious holidays observed.
Residence	ACCEPTABLE: Inquiries about the applicant's address needed for future contact with the applicant. INADVISABLE: Whether the applicant owns or rents own home (denotes economic class). Names or relationship of persons with whom applicant resides.
Sex	ACCEPTABLE: None. INADVISABLE: Any question.

Don't Call Us . . .

"Thanks so much for coming in. You'll hear from us one way or the other," Supervisor Philippe Velasquez said as he accompanied the applicant to the door.

His next interview was in 15 minutes with a woman named Paula Simpson. Personnel had given her high ratings, the supervisor recalled as he looked over her resume.

Dealing with Day-to-Day Supervisory Problems

The intercom buzzed: "Ms. Paula Simpson is here to see you."

Ten minutes early. He liked that.

"Tell her to come in, please."

Velasquez was impressed the minute he saw her. She seemed completely confident and poised in a situation that made most people extremely nervous.

"I noticed on your resume," Velasquez said after they'd talked for a few minutes, "that you did cold-canvas selling for two years. That's hard work."

"It is," Simpson replied. "When I got out of school, I wanted to try selling. Since I didn't have any experience, door-to-door selling was the only kind of job I could get. It went fairly well though. I actually made a living at it." She stopped and politely looked at the supervisor, waiting for the next question.

Door-to-door selling, Velasquez thought. No wonder she was so poised.

"You say it went fairly well . . ."

"Yes, it did. The reason I stopped was that I thought I'd like some kind of work where selling was a part of the job rather than the whole thing."

"I guess you know that's a pretty good description of the job we're trying to fill here. Have you any familiarity with legal language?"

"In my last job I worked for the head of a small business who happened to be a lawyer, so he drew up his own contracts. Working for him, I became pretty familiar with legal terminology."

"That's very important. We've found that if we can answer a customer's questions on the spot instead of having to call him back, it really helps."

"I know," Simpson said, smiling.

To Velasquez, Simpson seemed too good to be true. As Simpson sensed Velasquez's interest in her, she began to relax and the conversation became more chatty.

"My husband is a sales executive over at Apex. We used to trade selling tips."

"Sales executive?" Velasquez repeated "Gee, they get shifted around quite a bit, don't they? Do you know if your husband is subject to transfer?"

"I . . . I guess so," Simpson replied, losing her poise for the first time. "But I don't think it's going to happen very soon. We certainly haven't heard anything."

"I'd hate to break you in, then have to do it all over again with someone else in a year," Velasquez said, frowning.

"There really is nothing definite. It might not happen for years—if ever."

A few minutes later, Velasquez concluded the interview.

"We'll see what we can do," he said, noncommittally. "You'll hear from us within the next few weeks."

Two weeks later, Simpson got a letter thanking her for her time and expressing regret that the position had been filled.

RESULT: In a similar case, the woman filed a complaint with the EEOC, claiming that she'd been denied the job because of her sex. The EEOC supported her charge, saying that questions about family obligations ("Do you know if your husband is subject to transfer?") tend to have a *disparate effect*—in other words, a disproportionately large impact—on female applicants. Any employment practice that has a disparate effect on a protected class (women, blacks, etc.) is discriminatory and violates Title VII of the Civil Rights Act of 1964.

COMMENT: While it is important to ask male applicants the same questions you ask female applicants (and vice versa) there are some questions it is better not to ask at all—for example, questions about marital status, child care, family planning (asking applicants of child-bearing age if they might leave the job early to have children), etc. Here's why: Although asking both male and female applicants these questions *ap-*

pears to be fair, reality has shown that the answers to these questions *result* in limiting many women's employment opportunities while affecting few, if any, men. An employment practice that results in limiting the employment opportunities of one group more than others is said to have a *disparate effect* on that group and is therefore unlawful. The only exception to this is where the employment practice is a *business necessity,* something you must be prepared to prove (the burden of proof is on the employer) in court or before the EEOC.

The Royal Treatment

Supervisor Brad Corona was glad he'd gone over the job specifications. It had helped him narrow down the job qualifications until only one question remained, and that was how much on-the-job experience the applicant needed. Since Corona wasn't sure, he went to see his boss, Plant Manager Del Guttman.

"Del, I was just running down the specs for the technician's spot. The one thing I'm not sure about is whether or not completion of a one-year technician's training course is enough. Do you think they should also have on-the-job experience?"

"Of course," Guttman replied emphatically. "They must have at least *two years* experience. Whomever we hire has to be able to tune machinery on the spot. That means they'll have to have done the job before and learned to work under pressure. Besides, the schools train people on new equipment and a lot of our machinery is older."

"I guess you're right," Corona agreed. "Glad I asked."

As the supervisor began interviewing people for the spot, he was reminded that no minorities had ever held the technician's job before.

The fifth candidate he spoke to was Emma Dawes, a young black woman who'd gone back to school to get her technician's degree after working at assorted jobs for a number of years. Corona was impressed by her.

"How'd you like school?" he inquired.

"Pretty well, I guess. I finished first in my class."

Corona began to consider her as a serious candidate.

"I see you worked before you went to school. What exactly did you do?"

As Dawes began to describe her various jobs, Corona quickly realized that she had absolutely no experience as a technician. Despite her outstanding record at school, she really couldn't fill the bill.

Nevertheless, Corona was torn. She seemed so impressive.

Well, if she couldn't qualify for the technician's spot, maybe he could put her in as a technician's helper, a job that led to the technician's position, but paid about two-thirds the salary.

He didn't tell Dawes about his new idea, however. Since he liked her, he wanted her to like him and the company and to understand that the company was what it said it was: an equal opportunity employer.

So, he gave Dawes the royal treatment. He sent her around to be interviewed by the heads of those departments his department worked with.

One day, when he passed her in the hall after one of those interviews, he invited her back to his office for a cup of coffee when she was finished. Dawes accepted gratefully. She was obviously both pleased and flattered with the tremendous reception she was getting.

Later, while they were having coffee, Corona told her how the company had once been all white, and how it had changed drastically in recent years until there was now real opportunity for anyone with talent.

Dealing with Day-to-Day Supervisory Problems 19

"I have a feeling something will work out," the supervisor said confidently.

Dawes didn't say anything, but she had a mixed reaction to Corona's remark. On the one hand, he seemed very interested in her. After all, he'd sent her to see some key people. On the other hand, he'd just said he thought "something" would work out. Dawes wondered what he meant by that since she knew of only the one job opening.

One week later she got her answer by mail. A letter from the company offered her the job of technician's helper—at two-thirds the salary of the top spot for which she'd applied and been interviewed extensively.

When Dawes inquired as to why she hadn't been given the higher position, Corona explained that they'd never really considered her seriously for it because she lacked the crucial two years of experience.

But Dawes could not fit her V.I.P. treatment together with his explanation. In fact, the only conclusion she could come to was that they thought she was great, well-qualified, and a good prospective employee, but that they had dismissed these qualities in favor of a more important consideration: She was black.

RESULT: In a similar case, the individual filed suit, charging she'd been discriminated against because of her race. When the company was asked why she'd been interviewed so extensively if she simply wasn't qualified for the job, the supervisor explained that he'd really been trying to show her the genuineness of the company's EEO posture. However, in light of the fact that the top technician's spot had always been held by white males, his explanation seemed inadequate.

The company settled out of court for several thousand dollars. All things considered, the company may have gotten off at a relatively low cost.

COMMENT: Tell applicants the job specs and let them know whether or not they're qualified. If they have no chance for the job, don't waste your time and theirs by extending the interview process. In this case, the supervisor's efforts to show the company's posture on EEO was an effort to help the company at the expense of the applicant—even though he didn't intend it that way. Nobody likes to be built up for a letdown. Creating bitterness and a keen sense of injustice can hardly be considered "the royal treatment."

EVALUATION PRACTICES

Employee evaluations are an important part of nearly every important employment decision you make. For that reason your performance evaluations will be an important part of any investigation of discrimination charges.

Be sure that you evaluate employees only on the basis of job requirements and employee performance. Keep and use objective records of performance. Maintain a file of both positive and negative documentation of performance. Keep such a file on all employees, not only those with whom you anticipate trouble.

Challenge yourself on each rating and make sure you can justify it objectively. Have you established objective standards that can be applied to all employees holding that position? Have you evaluated on the basis of performance or on what you assume about an employee on the basis of job-unrelated characteristics?

If their performance doesn't merit it, don't give people a good evaluation to avoid "rocking the boat." Employees who get artificially high evaluations think they're doing a good job until they *don't* get a raise or promotion, or are fired. Then they assume they've been discriminated against on the basis of race, sex, or some other factor not related to performance. You'll have a difficult time proving otherwise, based on your "sugar coated" evaluations.

Give employees a realistic picture of the company policies on raises and promotions. Always solicit an employee's reaction to your evaluation. If there's disagreement, try to resolve it before the gap widens.

Everything's Coming Up Roses

It was evaluation time again and Supervisor Alex Lovitch's first performance review was with Bill Latham, a clerk in the Claims and Adjustments Department.

"Sit down, Bill," said Lovitch, as he closed his office door. "We'll try to make this as painless as possible." After a few pleasantries, Lovitch began. "I have to say you've sort of dropped off, performance-wise, over the last few months. Absent four times, late . . . two, three, four . . . well, I don't think I have to add them up for you. And, of course, there were those two cases that ended up in my lap."

Latham frowned. "I'm sorry, Al. I guess it's pretty bad."

"It's not that it's so bad. It's just way below what you're capable of. I keep telling you what great possibilities there are for you here, but you're not giving me anything I can put down on paper."

"I got the point."

"You understand that I'd be glad to help you out in any way I could."

"I understand," the clerk said quietly.

"I know what you can do, and what I should be able to expect of you—and that's what I'm going to demand of you. You had some nice raises your first few years, but I can't recommend you for one now. I have to draw the line somewhere. If you pick up, I can almost guarantee you a raise and maybe a promotion, too."

Then Lovitch went over Latham's record piece by piece, letting him know exactly which areas needed improvement.

"That's all the gory details I have for now," Lovitch concluded.

"It's enough for me."

"I hope it'll be a little easier next time."

Dealing with Day-to-Day Supervisory Problems 23

"Me, too."

After Latham had left, Lovitch sent for Ethel Monroe, one of the few black clerks in the department.

"Come in, come in," Lovitch said cheerfully. He always made a point of being as cheerful as possible around Monroe.

As he glanced over her record, however, he saw, to his dismay, that she hadn't improved her rather dismal performance. Her work was marginal at best. While her attendance was just about average she was late at least twice a week, and she needed so much supervision on the job that Lovitch thought of her as a perpetual trainee.

Still, the supervisor reflected, the company was strong on its Affirmative Action commitment and he did not want to be the one to make waves. Suppose Monroe got sore and filed a charge of discrimination against him? It just wasn't worth the hassle.

"Everything looks okay here," he said, glancing up and forcing a smile, hoping he didn't sound like he was lying through his teeth.

Monroe breathed a sigh of relief.

"I guess we could improve attendance a little, maybe watch the lateness from time to time. But over all, I'd say everything's going fine. Maybe we can even see about getting you a little more money."

The supervisor concluded the evaluation—Monroe's fourth good one in two years—then put off the rest of his interviews till afternoon.

A few months later a drastic drop in business resulted, first, in a hiring freeze, then, in lay-offs. Lovitch was told to cut six people in his department.

On the list that he compiled for Personnel, Monroe was at the top—the worst performer he had. He did not even consider putting Latham on the list because, to Lovitch's thinking, Latham was indispensable.

When Monroe received her pink slip, she was shocked. She'd only recently received her second raise in two years and had always had good evaluations. Her discharge could be the result of only one thing: racism. Lovitch, or the company—she didn't care which—was pulling an old trick: making blacks the last hired, and first fired.

She filed a charge of "discrimination because of race" with the EEOC.

RESULT: Although a similar case has not yet been decided, the EEOC is almost sure to find the company in violation of Title VII. It's all in the record. A black female employee with consistently good evaluations and two raises is fired while a white male employee with one or two mediocre evaluations and no recent raises is retained. If the supervisor testifies in his own defense that the evaluations are inaccurate and the EEOC asks him to explain why, what will he say? That he never bothered to criticize or correct the female employee's performance because she was black? Because he didn't want to "make waves?" Because he thought she was incapable of doing a decent job? Any such admissions would be stronger proof of discrimination than the discharge itself since they acknowledge both the supervisor's bias (he never even *tried* to improve her performance) and his discriminatory behavior (he gave her a certain kind of evaluation because she was black). In short, he is in an indefensible position.

COMMENT: What action should be taken when female and minority employees don't live up to your work standards? The same action you would take with white, male employees: tell them. Be tactful, but be honest. Explain where they need to improve and how much; whether they need more supervision or must do it on their own. When you whitewash poor performance you don't give people a chance to improve. In fact, your silence suggests that you don't think they *can* improve. You also limit your supervisory authority, because any future action you take will contradict earlier evaluations. Like the woman in this case, the female or minority (or older) employee who is first given good reviews for poor work and later fired can only conclude that the discharge is based on sex or race (or age).

The Vocal One

"Hey Milt," Service Supervisor Dennis Fields greeted Sales Supervisor Milt Danowitz, "you know that new girl in your department—I think she's a sales assistant—Virginia Poppolus? She any good?

"Nissen says she's super. So do the other salesmen. I've even had customers tell me about her."

"Well, I'm glad she's working out for you 'cause she sure is making *my* life miserable. It seems she has some girlfriends in my department and every time she comes to see them, *someone* asks me for a raise or promotion. She must be one of those real women's libbers. Can't you put a leash on her or something?"

"Sorry she's giving you a hard time," Danowitz replied, "I'll see what I can do." Although he decided he'd keep an eye on her, the supervisor wasn't really sure what he could do.

Over the next few weeks, he saw Poppolus talking to the other sales assistants. Her favorite topic was how the vast majority of sales people were men, but *all* the sales *assistants* were women.

One afternoon, Danowitz had a visitor.

"Can I see you?" said Sales Assistant Leslie Grogan after knocking on his door.

"What is it?" the supervisor asked.

"I'd like to become a saleswoman," she announced. "I've been here nearly four years." Danowitz could have fallen off his chair. Grogan was barely competent, the worst worker in the department.

"I see, I see," the supervisor said, trying to look as though he were weighing her request very seriously. "Do you really feel you're qualified, Leslie?"

"Well, just because I'm a woman doesn't mean I can't do a high-paying job!"

"Let me think about it."

Danowitz was positive that Poppolus had put Grogan up to it. Between Fields' being upset and Grogan's coming to see him, Danowitz was getting uneasy. It all came to a head when Poppolus asked to be promoted from sales assistant to "salesperson" as she put it.

"But you've only been here six months," the supervisor explained.

"Half of the guys who sell here started with *no* experience," she protested. "Besides, I can be trained. If I were a man I'd get the job in a minute with my ability—and you know it."

"We have women in our sales force."

"Three," Poppolus retorted.

When the inverview ended, Danowitz has all he could do to keep his temper. He realized that Poppolus was going to be very vocal about her rights and that she was already urging the other women to be more vocal, too. The supervisor decided that he was going to have to get Poppolus in line. To do that, he knew he'd have to have some tangible evidence to go on.

So, to make a good case, he began to document her performance, and to keep special records of her absenteeism and tardiness. He made special notes when her absences fell on a Friday or Monday.

When Poppolus was out several times and late a few others, he knew he was developing a reasonable strong case.

While he was doing this, two more letters came in from customers complimenting Poppolus on her performance. He put these in separate file.

On her first anniversary with the company, Poppolus came to see him.

"Well, I've been here a year now, Mr. Danowitz. You said six months wasn't long enough so I waited. I really would like to get into sales and I think I've proved myself. What do you think

Dealing with Day-to-Day Supervisory Problems 27

about my getting that promotion now?"

"With a record like this?" Danowitz replied, dropping Poppolus' absenteeism and tardiness record on the desk where she could see it. "I think you can consider yourself lucky if we just let you stay on."

RESULT: In a similar case, the employee filed a charge with the EEOC claiming she'd been denied a promotion because of her sex, and the EEOC investigated. When the manager involved was questioned, he acknowledged that after the woman had complained about women being discriminated against on the sales force "and account of her absenteeism and tardiness was kept . . . and notes were made as to when an absence fell on a Friday or Monday." The EEOC observed "no other employee's attendance was kept in this manner. Letters from Respondent's salesmen and customers complimenting Charging Party's good work were not placed in her personnel file. Equivalent letters were placed in the files of other employees. Information in the personnel files is used to evaluate employees for promotion. Respondent advances no reasonable explanation for this disparate treatment." The company, through the actions of its manager, was found in violation of Title VII.

COMMENT: Proper documentation is supposed to be objective, to reflect all aspects of an employee's performance, the good with the bad. Ideally, it should correspond to any actions taken for or against an employee by a supervisor. While it can be used as a defense against unjust charges of discrimination, or as a support for well-founded disciplinary decisions, documentation, like any supervisory tool, can become an instrument of discrimination when it's not used correctly. For example, it cannot, as Danowitz attempted, be used just "to make a good case" against someone. If that wasn't proof enough of discrimination, there was his lack of effort to change

Poppolus' behavior, to improve her absenteeism and tardiness record by bringing each incident to her attention and talking to her about it. Instead, he simply wrote them down until he'd gathered enough "evidence." It should be noted that when women have won class action suits against companies and been awarded money, the more vocal female employees have sometimes been awarded *extra* money because of the risks they incurred, and the strain they suffered, in being more vocal.

PROMOTION PRACTICES

The first step in deciding who to promote corresponds to the beginning of the hiring process. Take a good look at the job and decide what the *minimum* qualifications are. Identify any interchangable qualifications, such as education, experience, and training. Check the requirements you've determined against the qualifications of employees currently doing the job. If current employees don't meet the requirements and still do the job adequately, your standards are too high.

Next, it's important to evaluate *all* employees who meet those minimum standards. This requires informing all employees about the opening and encouraging everyone to apply, whether through a job posting system or by informally canvassing your department. If no women or minority employees apply, you must investigate and try to correct the situation.

From the pool of applicants, it's up to you to pick the most qualified for the promotion. This often involves subjective judgements. Be sure that those subjective criteria are essential to the performance of the job. Similarly, be sure that you can justify the person you choose as most qualified.

It is worthwhile to sit down afterwards with every employee who failed to qualify. A frank discussion of the reasons for the decision and the ways he or she can improve chances next time around (take a course, get more experience, improve performance, etc.) will help employees plan their careers, and may head off charges of discrimination.

The Last-Minute Qualification

On the average, Supervisor Harry Lundig had to promote two people a year from Customer Service Clerk to Customer Service Specialist. That was because every year, two Specialists were promoted to Sales.

Lundig's preliminary choices for this year were Mike Dougherty and Johnny Wesson. Although Lundig said nothing to anybody about his selections, word somehow got around that Dougherty and Wesson were the two clerks in the running.

One of the people who heard the news on the grapevine was Barbara Morris, a black clerk who'd been in the department eight years. She'd waited and waited for a promotion, but it had never come. Now, it seemed, she was going to miss it again.

"Mr. Lundig," Morris said one morning, after Lundig had given her her morning assignments, "I heard some more Specialist jobs may be opening up soon."

"I'd say that's a definite possibility, yes."

"Could I ask you what kind of qualifications a Service Clerk like myself might need to become a Service Specialist?"

"Well, three major considerations are seniority, education, and experience. There are other factors, too. Actually, if you'd like to know all of them, maybe we could talk about it in my office some time."

"I would appreciate it," Morris agreed.

Two days later, Morris found herself sitting in her supervisor's office, listening to him enumerate the qualifications for Customer Service Specialist. When he was through, Morris inquired about her personal standing.

"Let's have a look at your record," Lundig said, getting up. The supervisor got her record out and began to go over her seniority, education, and experience, as well as her performance. "You look good in all these areas," Lundig said, almost surprised. Morris had thought her record was good, but she was glad to hear Lundig confirm it. "Of course, I can't promise anything until I've gone over your record more carefully and looked at the records of the other people I'm considering, but you seem to be in good shape."

"Oh ... good. Do you know when you may be making a final decision?"

"Couple of weeks."

"Thanks for the time," Morris said on her way out.

"My door's always open."

Two weeks later Dougherty and Wesson were promoted to Customer Service Specialist; Morris, however, was not.

"Mr. Lundig, you said I was qualified," Morris objected after she'd heard the news. "I don't understand. I have more seniority and education than Dougherty and Wesson—and my experience is just as good."

"Barbara, as you know, some of our products are electrical and Mike and Johnny do have some familiarity with motors and electricity—more than you, I think."

"I never heard you had to know anything about motors or electricity to be a Specialist."

"I think it helps," Lundig said firmly.

"Why didn't you tell me that when we talked?"

"I should have, but to be honest, it slipped my mind. Anyway, I don't think you could have become familiar with those subjects in such a short time."

"I don't think you're leveling with me, Mr. Lundig. I think there's another problem."

"What do you mean, 'another problem'?"

"I mean I think there's a racial issue here."

"Now you *know* that doesn't make sense," Lundig said emphatically. "Of the 21 guys who are specialists, seven are black."

Morris was stunned: He was right—there were many black Customer Service Specialists. In her anger she had forgotten that. She didn't know what to say. Finally, she excused herself and left.

Morris didn't know what to make of the chain of events. Yet, the more she thought about it the more she could arrive at only one conclusion: Despite the number of blacks who held the Specialist job, she, Barbara Morris, had been denied the promotion because she was black.

She decided to file a complaint with the EEOC.

RESULT: In a similar case, the employee's charge of racial discrimination was not sustained. *But* the EEOC *did* find that "Reasonable cause exists to believe that Respondent Employer ... violated ... Title VII by denying Charging Party promotions *because of her sex*...." (Emphasis added.) The EEOC came to this conclusion after an investigation in which it found that "Charging Party was as qualified as male A, male B, and others holding the Customer Service Specialist position, that she had the background to be a good Customer Service Specialist [and] ... that experience with electricity and motors was not essential to effective performance as a Customer Service Specialist, since someone was always there who could answer difficult questions.... Accordingly, the policy pursuant to which Respondent denied Charging Party the promotion(s) ... was unlawful under Title VII."

COMMENT: Make sure your job descriptions include *only* those abilities, skills, and experience actually needed for the next job. If your job descriptions are out of date or contain irrelevant requirements, have these requirements removed or changed. Another point to be noted is that EEOC does not require that a complainant accurately describe the *kind* of discrimination he or she has suffered in order for the EEOC to find probable cause. In the case related above, when the EEOC found no probable cause that discrimination because of *race* existed, it didn't just drop the case. It continued its investigation until it discovered first *if* discrimination existed (which it did) and then what kind of discrimination was being practiced—discrimination because of sex.

By the Book

Supervisor Ed Reichold did things by the book. He prided himself on doing things "right." If he knew he was never going

Dealing with Day-to-Day Supervisory Problems 33

to win any popularity contests in his shipping and receiving department, he also knew that he'd had fewer personnel problems than many of the other supervisors.

A number of his employees griped about how rigid he was in sticking to company rules and procedures, but no one had gone over Reichold's head during the last few years and he'd had few requests for transfers.

The small number of personnel problems Reichold had encountered was particularly impressive in light of the diversity of his workforce: one third of the material handlers were black and three quarters were women.

When the company implemented a new EEO policy and hired an EEO officer to help administer it, the only thing that concerned Reichold was how promotions would be handled.

The rigorous new procedures required for promotion recommendations didn't bother the supervisor. It was the conflicts that Reichold feared might occur when minorities, women, and white males all bid for the same jobs.

However, as it turned out, his anxieties were unfounded. The fact was, few minority or female employees had bid for promotions under the company's job posting system.

One morning, Reichold noticed that a job opening for group leader had been posted. It was one of the slots that had remained completely white-male.

So Reichold was pleased when Betty Franklin, one of his black material handlers, bid for the job.

Unfortunately, she was the only black or female employee in his department to bid. The other eight bidders were all white males.

Reichold methodically reviewed the record of each bidder, comparing it to the company's requirements for the group leader job.

There were some minimal experience/training requirements: demonstrated ability to work closely with others, to give orders and to evaluate others' work, and attendance/punctuality standards that the candidate had to meet.

Franklin had a good record and was qualified in all areas but one—she had neither training nor experience in operating the machinery used on the loading dock.

In keeping with company policy, Riechold called her in for an individual counseling session to tell her that she had not qualified and what she had to do in order to qualify for the next opening.

"You've got a good record, Betty," Reichold told the materials' handler. "The only thing you lack is experience with the machinery."

"Does that mean you're not recommending me for the promotion?" Franklin retorted.

"I can't. Look," the supervisor said, coming around his desk with the company specs in his hand, "see these qualifications? You've got to have some kind of training or experience with the forklifts, the cranes, and the other machinery."

"I keep hearing about all the opportunity this company offers but I never see any of it. I really don't," Franklin said.

"That's not true," Reichold argued. "In fact, I was going to tell you that I personally will give you the training you need and within a few months you'll be qualified for group leader. If your record remains as good as it is now, I'll be happy to recommend you."

"I don't know what to think," Franklin replied. "I believe you, but I simply haven't seen any women or black people in those group leader jobs. Did you recommend any?"

"The truth is, Betty, you're the only woman or black employee who bid."

"Mm. Well, I can understand that," Franklin commented.

Reichold wasn't sure exactly what she meant, but he let it go.

Within a few months, Reichold found out that Franklin had filed a discrimination charge, claiming that the company discriminated in its promotion policies "as evidenced by its failure to promote minorities and women."

While she didn't hold the supervisor personally responsible, she did say he was part of the problem, since he hadn't recommended any black or female employees for promotion to group leader.

RESULT: In a similar case, the EEOC found the company in violation of Title VII for failing to make its own investigation into why women and minorities had consistently failed to bid for promotions. The government's inquiry revealed a general feeling of disillusionment among black and female employees who, having seen other blacks and females bid for promotions and not get them, had concluded that the bidding system was a waste of time—at least for minorities and women.

While the company's personnel department and EEO coordinator bore some of the responsibility for not having made a better evaluation of the company's promotion program, the EEOC decision might have gone the other way had the supervisor in this case kept track of who was bidding for promotions *and* talked to those many blacks and women who never bid to find out why they hadn't.

COMMENT: If you find that none of the minority or female employees are bidding for promotions, find out why. Then do whatever is needed to convince them that they have as much chance to get ahead as white male employees. This kind of affirmative effort is just as much your legal responsibility under Title VII as making unbiased promotion recommendations. To put it another way, fair and objective evaluation of your promotion process is as important as fair evaluation of the employees who bid for promotions.

DISCIPLINE PRACTICES

If you are forced to discipline employees, use the same standard that applies to other employment practices. Administer the same punishment for the same infraction to all offenders.

Be prepared to justify your disciplinary actions. Know all the facts regarding the incident and be able to document them. Who was involved? Who witnessed the incident? What happened? What led up to it? Where did it happen? Why did it happen? Why did you take the action you did? Etc.

Check to see what disciplinary action you took other times a similar incident took place. Be sure that the employee's record warrants the severity of the punishment.

"Why Me?"

Earl Johnson didn't mind being the only black employee in his department. The unit was small and, except for some bad vibes from his supervisor, Jim Dunlop, Johnson found it a nice place to work.

Johnson was out one Tuesday. When he returned to work on Wednesday, Dunlop said angrily, "You're late."

"I'm sorry," said Johnson, taking a quick look around. Only about half the department was there. Johnson knew that of those who still hadn't arrived, many wouldn't be coming in at all. That was the way the department ran. So why, Johnson reflected, was Dunlop picking on him?

"By the way," said the supervisor, "where were you yesterday?"

"Out," said Johnson. He'd never heard Dunlop ask anyone for an excuse.

Dealing with Day-to-Day Supervisory Problems 37

"I know you were out. *Why* were you out?"

Johnson hesitated. "Personal business."

Dunlop let it go at that, but from then on the supervisor bore down on Johnson. Every time he called Johnson on something, Johnson wanted to say, "Everybody else does it," but he didn't think that was a good excuse. Besides, he didn't want the other people in the department to think that he was trying to get them in trouble.

A few weeks later, Dunlop wrote him up for being late, and then again for being absent.

"Hey, what is this?" Johnson demanded.

"What do you mean, *'what is this'?*" Dunlop retorted. "It's progressive discipline. I've given you some verbal warnings, now I'm giving you some written warnings and the next time you're late or absent, I'm going to suspend you."

"But why me?" Johnson protested.

"Because you're late or absent all the time."

"That's not true. Besides, there are at least four white employees here with worse attendance records than mine. How come you don't lean on them?"

"It's my job to enforce the rules around here and it's your job to obey them. If you don't, I have a right to do something about it. You have no beef."

"You can't apply the rules to only me."

"Like I said," Dunlop replied, "the next time you slip, you're suspended."

RESULT: Here's what the EEOC ruled in a similar case: "Statements of numerous ... employees ... indicate that supervision ... was very lax ... that the complainant's performance was not significantly different from that of ... fellow employees ... Time cards indicate that at least one Caucasian who worked under the same Supervisor was absent considerably more often than [the complainant]. From the witnesses' testimony ... we can only conclude that the disparity was due to ... race. Reasonable cause exists to believe that the supervisor engaged in unlawful employment practices ... by discriminating against the employee ... because of race...."

COMMENT: Documentation—writing down incidents that reflect on an employee's performance—and progressive discipline are both good supervisory techniques. But these, like all supervisory practices, must be applied equally to all employees regardless of race, color, religion, sex or national origin. If you use them as a weapon against a specific individual or group, you may be responsible for involving your company in a lengthy investigation or even a possible court suit.

The Record Speaks For Itself

"Louise," Processing Supervisor Lillian Loeb said to her clerk, Louise Wilson, "I'm giving you back these five address-correction slips. You forgot to put in the zip codes again. This is the third time in two days I've had to remind you. I shouldn't have to do that."

"How come you're always criticizing me?" Wilson snapped. "How can a person get anything done when they're always being picked on?"

"I'm not picking on you," Loeb said patiently. "The fact is you make too many mistakes—more than anyone else here and, frankly, more than are acceptable. If you don't believe me, I'll let you see your weekly performance record. Unless your work improves, I'm afraid I'll have to let you go. You've had plenty of warning."

Loeb knew that even though the department was half black and there had been no problems or complaints, Wilson was convinced she was being discriminated against because she was black.

Dealing with Day-to-Day Supervisory Problems

And Loeb was not immune to Wilson's remarks. In fact, they unnerved her. The supervisor went back to her office and ran through the previous week's performance records. Yes, she'd been right. None of her employees—black or white—had a record like Wilson's. And the clerk had had numerous warnings. The well-documented performance records reassured Loeb that the problem was Wilson's and not her's.

The next morning, Loeb's department manager came to see her.

"Lil, I think these came from one of your people," he said, handing her a stack of red-inked tickets. "Not only are the addresses wrong, a few have the wrong phone numbers, too. It took us several days to track down these people and we still haven't been able to locate two of them."

"I'm sorry," Loeb said, embarrassed. "It won't happen again."

She recognized the work as Wilson's.

"Louise, I believe you filled out these forms, didn't you?" the supervisor asked as she approached Wilson's desk. "They have your number on them."

"Well, if you know they're mine, why are you asking?"

Loeb was determined not to lose her temper.

"This is your final warning," the supervisor said quietly. "Your work is really unacceptable. The next time you make more than ten mistakes in a week—and that's way over the department average—I'm going to have to let you go."

"I bet I wouldn't be fired if I was white," Wilson countered.

"The person you were hired to replace was white," Loeb explained. "And we let her go for the same reason—she just wasn't doing the job. I've given you every chance."

"You mean you've taken every chance to supervise me to death. I must be the most supervised person in this place."

"If you want to see less of me, just make fewer mistakes. You've had your last warning."

But the following week her work was even worse. She made over ten mistakes before the week was even half over. When Loeb told Wilson she'd been terminated, the clerk angrily replied, "I never had a chance with you supervising me every minute. Nobody can do a job when they're leaned on like that."

RESULT: In a similar case, an employee who'd been fired filed a complaint with the EEOC, charging that the termination had been based on race. The EEOC investigated and rendered the following decision: "Half of Respondent's forty (40) employees are Negro. There is no evidence in the record that Charging Party in particular or Negro employees as a class received more . . . supervision than did Caucasian [employees]. Accordingly, we do not find a reasonable basis for crediting the charge. Reasonable cause does not exist to believe that the [employee's] charge was true."

COMMENT: The supervisor came out of this investigation unscathed. Here's why: First, the supervisor had well documented records of every employee's performance. The documentation served to prove that the discharge was based on objective evidence and not on bias. Second, the supervisor followed past practice for, as Loeb explained to Wilson, she had been hired to replace a white employee fired for the same reason—poor performance. Last, the EEOC's statement that "There is no evidence in the record that . . . Negro [employees] as a class received more supervision than did Caucasian [employees] . . ." indicates that when black employees in the department were interviewed by the EEOC investigators, they corroborated the supervisor's contention of fair and impartial supervision and not the employee's contention of supervisory bias.

Distinction Without a Difference

Ever since Warehouse Supervisor Ken Herman had been able to get a couple of forklift trucks and some extra skids, the loaders' job had become a lot easier. They even found themselves with some idle time on their hands.

"Johnny," Loader Brian Stone said to John Webbing, a co-worker, "I gotta do something this afternoon. Punch out for me, will ya?"

Webbing hesitated, then said, "Sure."

At the end of the shift, Webbing punched out, kneeled down to tie his shoe while he looked around, then quickly grabbed Stone's card and punched it.

He was about to replace the card in the rack when he heard a voice: "What do you think you're doing?" It was Ken Herman, Webbing's supervisor.

"Huh? Oh . . . I . . . ah . . ."

"First thing tomorrow morning—in my office. You and Stone."

The following morning Herman chewed them both out and warned them that next time it happened he'd fire them. Neither Webbing nor Stone protested and neither mentioned the incident to the union rep.

Hector Fernandez stood on the loading dock watching some freight cars roll down the siding and onto a feeder track. As he turned to go back into the warehouse, he bumped into Rafael Navarro, a friend and co-worker.

"Say, Raf, you gonna watch the game tonight?" Fernandez asked.

"If I can get my T.V. back, I am," Navarro replied. "The shop said it was fixed; all I have to do is pick it up. Hey, maybe you could do me a favor."

"Sure. What is it?"

"If I wait till the end of the shift to pick up the T.V., I won't get home until 7 o'clock. The repair place is right in the middle of town. But if I leave early, I can beat the rush. Could you punch me out? There's nothing left for me to do today, anyway."

"No sweat," Fernandez replied.

But when Fernandez went to punch Navarro out, one of the supervisors caught him and immediately reported the incident to Ken Herman. This time, Herman really hit the ceiling. The next morning he had both Fernandez and Navarro in his office—with a union rep.

When Fernandez and Navarro left the supervisor's office, they had pink slips; they'd been fired. The union contract, Herman explained, specifically stated that if one employee punched out for another, both could be fired.

Although the supervisor saw it as a cut-and-dried issue, Navarro and Fernandez did not. They filed a complaint with the EEOC claiming that they were discharged because they were of Mexican extraction. As proof of their allegation, they related the incident in which Webbing had punched out for Stone and the two Anglo employees had received only a reprimand. Such unequal treatment of identical infractions, the two discharged Spanish-surnamed employees charged, was proof that their terminations had been discriminatory.

RESULT: In a similar case, the employer contended that the two Anglo employees had only been reprimanded because they had not left the premises (something the employer could not prove and which witnesses contradicted), but that the two Spanish-surnamed employees had been discharged because they had left the premises and by doing so were "defrauding" the company. The EEOC, however, ruled that the employer was seeking "to rely upon a distinction without a difference. Plainly, all four employees were involved in action which 'defrauded' the employer of payment for services not rendered. Accordingly, the only difference discernible between the two sets of guilty employees is their respective national origin." The employer was found in violation of Title VII.

COMMENT: Before carrying out any serious disciplinary action—written warning, suspension, discharge—against minority or female employees, double-check to make sure that you have taken similar action against Anglo, male employees for similar offenses. If you fail to take this extra precaution, and it turns out (as it did in the case above) that similar action was not taken against Anglo employees for a similar offense, you'll have no defense should the minority or female employee file a complaint. Did Supervisor Herman fire Navarro and Fernandez because they were of Mexican extraction? Or did he fire them because they were the second pair he'd caught violating the rule? The fact is, it doesn't matter what his reasons were. The EEOC is interested in the *results* of an employer's action—not the intent.

EMPLOYEES FILING CHARGES

An employee who accuses you or your organization of discrimination or testifies against you in a hearing or court case cannot be punished, intimidated, disciplined, or otherwise harassed for doing so.

Retaliation charges filed during the investigation of an earlier discrimination charge may have more merit than the original complaint. In addition, the company may find its position on the original charge weakened by a supervisor's subsequent conduct.

The basic guideline for dealing with an employee after he or she has filed a discrimination charge is to treat that employee as if no charge was filed. While this may be very difficult to put into practice, it is your best protection against retaliation or intimidation charges. Anything even *appearing* to be done to punish the employee for making the charge while it is being investigated may be interpreted as retaliation by a hypersensitive employee (and the Court).

While it is important not to cut off normal communication with the employee, it is in your best interest *not* to discuss the discrimination charge. Avoid any jokes or comments which you may consider tension-relievers, but which the employee may see as further evidence of discrimination and which can be used in Court.

These guidelines apply for supervising an employee who has filed a discrimination charge whether the charge is specifically against you or is a charge against the company.

What Does the EEOC Actually Do When A Complaint Is Filed?

If none of your employees has ever filed a discrimination complaint against you, chances are you've never seen the

Dealing with Day-to-Day Supervisory Problems

EEOC's "Charge of Discrimination" form. Reproduced in its entirety on page 46, the whole form covers just one side of an 8½ x 11 sheet.

If one of your employees were to fill the form out and mail it to the EEOC, or go to a branch office to seek help in filling it out, the first thing the Commission would do is make sure that the alleged discrimination was because of race, sex, creed, color, or national origin and not discrimination because of age or handicaps which is handled by other agencies.

Once the EEOC had decided the complaint was within its jurisdiction, it would immediately... defer the charge to a state or local government agency. That's not bureaucratic buck-passing and it's not courtesy—it's the law. Congress built this "automatic deferral" into Title VII (Section 706) because it wanted problems worked out, if possible, at the local level, and for the federal government to be called in only if the state or local agencies failed to resolve the complaint.

WHO'S WHO? The person who files the complaint is known as the "Charging Party" (CP) and the organization against which the charge is filed (company, state government employer, local government employer) is called the "Respondent."

Once the EEOC has deferred the charge, it will not take any action until—

(1) the CP has received a final determination—i.e., verdict—from the state or local government agency, or,
(2) the CP has spent at least 60 days trying to settle the problem through the state or local government agency.

Although technically the EEOC takes over jurisdiction of a case on the 61st day, it will usually wait for the local agency to give its determination before it acts.

The EEOC reviews the state or local agency's findings to see whether it will accept or reject those findings. Should the EEOC reject the local agency's determination and decide to

(PLEASE PRINT OR TYPE)

CHARGE OF DISCRIMINATION	EEOC CHARGE NO.	FORM APPROVED OMB NO. 124-R0001

INSTRUCTIONS	CAUSE OF DISCRIMINATION
If you have a complaint, fill in this form and mail it to the Equal Employment Opportunity Commission's District Office in your area. In most cases, a charge must be filed with the EEOC within a specified time after the discriminatory act took place. IT IS THEREFORE IMPORTANT TO FILE YOUR CHARGE AS SOON AS POSSIBLE. *(Attach extra sheets of paper if necessary.)*	☐ RACE OR COLOR ☐ SEX ☐ RELIGIOUS CREED ☐ NATIONAL ORIGIN

NAME *(Indicate Mr. or Ms.)*		DATE OF BIRTH
STREET ADDRESS	COUNTY	SOCIAL SECURITY NO.
CITY, STATE, AND ZIP CODE		TELEPHONE NO. *(Include area code)*

THE FOLLOWING PERSON ALWAYS KNOWS WHERE TO CONTACT ME

NAME *(Indicate Mr. or Ms.)*	TELEPHONE NO. *(Include area code)*
STREET ADDRESS	CITY, STATE, AND ZIP CODE

LIST THE EMPLOYER, LABOR ORGANIZATION, EMPLOYMENT AGENCY, APPRENTICESHIP COMMITTEE, STATE OR LOCAL GOVERNMENT WHO DISCRIMINATED AGAINST YOU *(If more than one, list all)*

NAME	TELEPHONE NO. *(Include area code)*
STREET ADDRESS	CITY, STATE, AND ZIP CODE

OTHERS WHO DISCRIMINATED AGAINST YOU *(If any)*	

CHARGE FILED WITH STATE/LOCAL GOV'T. AGENCY ☐ YES ☐ NO	DATE FILED	AGENCY CHARGE FILED WITH *(Name and address)*
APPROXIMATE NO. OF EMPLOYEES/MEMBERS OF COMPANY OR UNION THIS CHARGE IS FILED AGAINST		DATE MOST RECENT OR CONTINUING DISCRIMINATION TOOK PLACE *(Month, day, and year)*

Explain what unfair thing was done to you and how other persons were treated differently. Understanding that this statement is for the use of the United States Equal Employment Opportunity Commission, I hereby certify:

I swear or affirm that I have read the above charge and that it is true to the best of my knowledge, information and belief.		SUBSCRIBED AND SWORN TO BEFORE ME THIS DATE *(Day, month, and year)*
DATE	CHARGING PARTY *(Signature)*	
Subscribed and sworn to before this EEOC representative.		SIGNATURE *(If it is difficult for you to get a Notary Public to sign this, sign your own name and mail to the District Office. The Commission will notarize the charge for you at a later date.)*
DATE	SIGNATURE AND TITLE	

NOTARY PUBLIC

EEOC FORM JUN 72 5   Previous editions of this form may be used.

Dealing with Day-to-Day Supervisory Problems 47

investigate the case itself, it will send the Respondent a form letter within 10 days stating the basis of the discrimination charge—race, color, creed, or national origin—and the issues involved—discharge, discipline, promotion, etc. The case then goes to the "pending investigation" section, until an investigator has been assigned, a process that may take anywhere from a few weeks to a year.

THE INVESTIGATION BEGINS. When the investigator is assigned, the Respondent receives an exact copy of the "Charge of Discrimination." The investigator's first job is to get all the facts he can from the state or local agency that first reviewed the case, and then to seek any additional information he may need by interviewing the CP, witnesses and company representatives. The investigator will also ask for pertinent documentation such as EEO-1 reports, lists of recent promotions, demotions, discharges, a copy of the labor-management agreement (if the company has a union), personnel files, etc. The EEOC can go to court if this information is not given upon request.

SUPPOSE THE COMPLAINT NAMES YOU. Naturally, when the "Charge" form asks the CP to "Explain what unfair thing has been done to you and how other persons were treated differently," names may be named. The EEOC, however, encourages people *not* to mention names on the Charge form, but to give them only to the investigator in confidential testimony. And even if your name were mentioned, it's Commission policy not to go after *people* but to investigate organizations, and to let the organization which has been charged pick whom it wishes to represent it: attorneys, EEO managers, personnel or plant managers, etc.

In fact, in its initial communication with a company, an EEOC investigator may simply call and tell the switchboard operator that a charge of discrimination has been filed and ask to be put through to the person who handles the organization's EEO responsibilities.

If the investigator wants to interview you, he'll make an appointment to see you. You may be interviewed alone or with a personnel manager, department head, or other representative of your organization.

Generally, the investigator will take notes on what you say, but you are not under oath and will not be asked to sign a statement unless he thinks he needs a sworn affidavit. You will not know what the Charging Party or witnesses have told the investigator, nor will they know what you say. All testimony is confidential.

Every investigator works closely with an EEOC supervisor during an investigation. At the investigation's conclusion, the investigator writes up a memo saying whether or not he thinks there is probable cause to believe that discrimination exists. This memo goes to the EEOC's district director who makes the final ruling which in most cases goes along with the investigator's decision.

The district director sends the CP and Respondent a *determination,* i.e. the Commission's findings regarding the charge, which would look something like this:

"Mr. John Doe, Charging Party vs. Alphabet Motor Corp. Mr. John Doe claims he was discriminated against in not being promoted because he was black. The record shows that there are X number of employees at Alphabet Motors and that Y number of these employees are black. The record shows that while three white workers from John Doe's department and eight white workers from other departments were promoted within the last four months, only two black employees were promoted within the company during the same time period. Based on the above I (investigator) find (there is/there is not) probable cause to believe that discrimination exists." If there is a finding of *no* probable cause, the CP still has the right to ask, in writing, for authorization to sue the Respondent in Federal District Court.

Dealing with Day-to-Day Supervisory Problems

WHEN THERE IS PROBABLE CAUSE. If the charge is upheld, the EEOC district director will have a "conciliator" (usually the investigator who has handled the case) confer with the CP and Respondent to reach an agreement that is acceptable to both parties and which complies with the law. Although both parties may designate whom they please to draw up the conciliation agreement, it's generally done by lawyers since a conciliation agreement is a quasi-legal document.

After the agreement has been put in writing, it is approved by the EEOC's district director and signed by the CP and Respondent.

If the parties cannot agree, the Commission may sue to enforce compliance with the law. If the EEOC decides not to sue, or if the EEOC has not finally resolved the charge within 180 days, the CP may request written authorization to sue.

ARE REPUTATIONS AT STAKE? Yes and no. Unless a case has been filed in court no employee of the EEOC may make any part of a complaint public in any way. This includes all information provided by the charging party, by the organization charged, by witnesses, etc. The CP and Respondent themselves, however, are *not* bound by any rules of confidentiality.

JUSTICE TAKES TIME. The EEOC acknowledges that all this may seem long-winded. But it is the very lengthiness of the process, the Commission contends, that ensures that the rights and interests of all parties are protected and that every opportunity is made available to settle discrimination complaints *without* the necessity of a court trial.

Leave Well Enough Alone

"I still don't see why I have to do all the dirty work," Flora Nash, the new black typist in the department, complained. She was angry at having to do what seemed to her an unfair share of the menial tasks—cleaning the coffee-maker, straightening the supply cabinet, etc.

"I told you already," her supervisor, Ben Whittaker replied, "the new people always do those jobs."

"That's not what I heard."

"What do you mean?"

"I mean I heard you used to spread the dirty work around."

"That's right, we *used* to spread it around," Whittaker agreed, "but that was two years ago, long before you got here. We dropped the old system because it got *everyone* upset. We decided it was fairer just to give it to the new people."

"Especially certain kinds of new people," Nash said bitingly.

"Everybody—black or white—gets the same treatment from me," Whittaker said quietly, trying to control his anger.

"All I know is I'm doing an awful lot of dirty work."

A few days later, Whittaker happened to be in another part of the building when he noticed Flora Nash standing in front of an EEO poster copying down some information. Whittaker knew that the only information on the poster was the address and phone number of the nearest place to file discrimination complaints.

He returned to his department very much upset. He decided to confront Nash right away. He asked her to come to his office.

"I want to talk to you about something that happened this morning . . ." he began.

"I'm doing my job," Nash said defensively.

"It's not about your job," Whittaker replied, "it's about something else. I was on the third floor this morning and I believe I saw you copying down some information from the EEO poster."

"Well . . . I think . . ." the typist stammered, afraid to say anything. "I think I have a right to do that . . ."

"Of course you do," Whittaker agreed. "But I think it would be pretty unfair to go filing a complaint of discrimination against me without at least talking to me first, don't you?"

"Who said I was going to file a complaint?" Nash said.

"Well, *whatever* you wanted that information for, I think you should know that I'm going to make a little note of your action and of our discussion here."

"But I haven't done anything," Nash protested.

"I didn't say you had," Whittaker replied.

"You're trying to intimidate me," Nash retorted, "and I won't let you do it."

RESULT: In a similar case, the employee filed a complaint with the EEOC, which investigated the case and rendered the following decision: "It has been the Commission's experience that an employee who is questioned in this way subjectively feels intimidated. . . Evidence indicates that [the employer's] supervisory personnel . . . engaged in intimidation in violation of Title VII. . ."

COMMENT: Here's what the EEOC is saying: The law states that employees have a right to file complaints of discrimination with the EEOC. *Any effort on the part of the supervisor—or any other member of management—to ask the employee about the filing of a possible complaint amounts to intimidation.* And intimidation is a violation of Title VII of the Civil Rights Act of 1964. The only thing you can do something about is the conditions which might lead to a complaint. Then, if the complaint is filed, at least you'll be on the right end of the EEOC's decision.

Part Two

There are certain groups with long histories of job discrimination. Some of the government regulations for ensuring equal employment opportunity were drafted specifically to protect employees from discrimination on the basis of sex, race, national origin, religion, age, or physical handicap.

The following section focuses on each of these types of discrimination by identifying common problems, providing some guidelines for action and examining actual cases. It also examines a new phenomenon brought about by affirmative action—reverse discrimination.

SEX DISCRIMINATION

Despite dramatic advances by women in the past ten years, thousands still face employment discrimination on the basis of their gender. As more women learn not to expect anything less than their male counterparts, more companies will be called upon to answer sex discrimination charges.

Examine your attitudes about women. Don't assume a woman job applicant can't or won't want to travel, work late, get her hands dirty, or do anything else a man does. Identify what you've always thought of as "men's jobs" and "women's jobs," and recognize that according to the law, virtually no jobs are defined by sex.

Give women a fair share of challenging tasks, but don't set up a woman for failure by assigning a weak female employee to heavy physical work on the pretext of "treating her like any other employee." Assign tasks to all employees on the basis of their abilities.

Resist the common tendency to automatically ask female employees, regardless of their level within your company, to get coffee, clean up, order lunch, or take minutes at a meeting. If those tasks are part of the job, tell the applicant so before hiring.

Avoid anything that would justify charges of sexual harassment. Beyond that, maintain an atmosphere free of intimidation and harassment. This means encouraging cooperation from male employees *and* from tradition-oriented female employees.

Who's Doing the Dirty Work?

Ann Walinski enjoyed the variety of her work; one week she was writing operating instructions for customers, the next, repair manuals for Maintenance.

Dealing with Day-to-Day Supervisory Problems

Although technical writing had previously been regarded as strictly men's work, she knew her being hired for the job indicated a change in the company's policy.

"Ann," Supervisor Paul Rahim said one afternoon, "could you refile these old manuals when you have a chance?"

"Sure," Walinski said cheerfully. "Say, didn't I just see these somewhere?" she asked, flipping through one of the booklets.

"Leo was using them this morning. He's through with them now."

"Oh . . . I see." But she didn't see. If Leo had been using them, she thought, why couldn't Leo refile them himself? That's certainly what she was expected to do. Walinski decided to let it go.

"Liked your intro for the LR-500 instructions," Rahim commented one afternoon. "Well organized. Had a little zip to it."

"Thanks. I had to rewrite it four or five times before it came out right."

"The work shows. Now, I have something I want you to do," he said, dropping some papers on her desk. "These customers wrote us some questions about the NDR instructions. I had Charlie write up the answers. I'd like you to type the letters and send them out. Here are the addresses and some letterheads with carbons. File the copies in Customer Service Correspondence."

"Look, I'm not afraid of hard work," Walinski replied, "but since Charlie wrote the answers, wouldn't *he* be the best person to write the letters?"

"I can't ask the guys to do secretarial stuff," Rahim said, surprised. "You wouldn't expect them to do clerical jobs when they're writers, would you?"

Walinski wanted to say "You know, I'm a writer too!" but she couldn't get up the nerve. She was sure Rahim would think an answer like that was hostile—if not insubordinate. She felt victimized. To keep her job as a skilled technical writer she had to work considerably beneath her ability and experience.

During the next few months, more and more of the clerical tasks seemed to find their way to Walinski's desk. She was just working herself up to complain about it when she received her semiannual evaluation—and no raise.

"But Leo and Charlie both got raises," she said to Rahim after he'd given her the bad news.

"That's true," he agreed, "but you do a lot of clerical work and you're being paid a writer's salary. You should be happy you're not being asked to take a cut."

RESULT: In a similar case, the EEOC noted the "puzzling circumstances which resulted in a woman of Charging Party's abilities and experience becoming burdened with clerical duties while male employees with less editorial and writing experience remained free from such duties .... Equal employment opportunity requires that an employer judge employees on the basis of individual merit not upon stereotyped concepts of 'female jobs' .... It is plain that Charging Party was placed in a disadvantaged position because of her sex." The EEOC concluded that the employer had violated Title VII.

COMMENT: Good employee relations have always required that no one person or group do all the unpleasant jobs. EEO laws have put teeth in this humane concept: It is now simply illegal to give minority or female workers all the menial or lower status chores. (It is also illegal to give male employees a raise, but deny a raise to female employees who do equally good work, as in the case above, since this amounts to discrimination in the "terms and conditions of employment," a violation of Title VII.) When male employees object to doing what they regard as "women's work," don't make it a male-female issue; instead, appeal to their sense of fairness: "Sure, typing (or filing, or cleaning the coffee pot) is a lousy job. But why should Alice do all the dirty work?"

Who's Embarrassed?

"Good morning. May I help you?" Carol Chevrier inquired cheerfully.

"Mr. Perrin, please?" one of the three men standing before her desk replied. "He's expecting us."

"And you are . . . ?"

"We're from Verentrix Corporation."

Chevrier dialed the extension and soon Perrin's secretary, Dotty Limon, appeared.

"Right this way, gentlemen," said Limon. As the men started through the doorway, Limon turned to Chevrier and patted her stomach. "How's it going?" she whispered.

"Four months," Chevrier whispered back.

Chevrier was referring to the fact that she was in the fourth month of her pregnancy. As she watched Limon disappear through the doorway, she thought about how glad she was to be working instead of just sitting home and waiting. Of course it was more than simply having something to do; Chevrier loved her job and wanted to keep at it as long as possible.

Chevrier had not yet told her boss that she was pregnant, but she knew she couldn't wait much longer. On her way back from lunch she stopped in to see him.

"Have a minute?" she inquired after knocking on his door.

"You bet," Supervisor Will Trafari replied. "Come on in."

"I thought you might like to know," Chevrier said after she was seated, that, well .. I'm expecting."

"Wonderful, Carol. I'm delighted. I have to be honest with you, it's not exactly news to me. I guess things get around here. Naturally, I didn't want to say anything until you told me yourself. Congratulations."

"Thanks," said Chevrier, pleased by his tactfulness.

"Actually, even if no one had said anything, I might have been able to figure it out pretty soon."

"The only reason I didn't tell you earlier," Chevrier explained, "was that . . . I don't know . . . I didn't want it to affect my job. I was planning to give you two months notice, but I'd hoped to stay on the job as long as possible."

"Absolutely," Trafari agreed. "In fact, I'm one step ahead of you there. I thought you'd probably want to work as long as possible, so I went ahead and arranged a transfer to the steno pool for you. No hurry, of course. You can finish out the month where you are. Looks to me like you'll be all right until then," he commented, glancing at her stomach.

"Transfer to the steno pool?" Chevrier repeated. She couldn't believe it. "Is there some problem? Something I'm doing wrong?"

"Of course not, Carol," Trafari said reassuringly. "It's just that . . . well, there's only one way to get in this building—through the front door. That means that everyone who comes here—customers, salespeople, visitors, you name it—has to walk past your desk. You shouldn't have to feel like you're in a goldfish bowl. By letting you spend your last few months in the steno pool we can avoid unnecessary embarrassment all around."

Embarrassment! Chevrier wondered. What was embarrassing about being pregnant? However, since Trafari had already arranged her transfer to Steno, she feared any resistance on her part might jeopardize her working altogether.

It was only when she found out she'd be working for less money in Steno that she decided to see a lawyer.

RESULT: Should Chevrier end up filing a complaint with the EEOC or starting a law suit, it would be very difficult for Trafari or company officials to prove—and that's what they would have to do, *prove*—that a pregnant employee's visibility to the public (customers, salespeople, visitors, etc.) substantially affects "the safe and efficient conduct of the business." And if they couldn't prove it, the company might be liable for backpay, attorney's fees, and possibly even damages.

Dealing with Day-to-Day Supervisory Problems

COMMENT: Unless an employee's pregnancy substantially affects her performance, threatens her safety or the safety of others, or interferes in some other way with the "safe and efficient conduct" of your department, think twice about taking any action that would affect the "terms and conditions" of her employment. Many supervisors, particularly male supervisors, have gotten their companies in big trouble by acting on the common but incorrect assumption that when a woman becomes pregnant she should be removed—fired, transferred, furloughed, etc.—from any job in which she might have contact with the public.

Wining and Dining

"Congratulations, Hal," Roslyn Jacobs said, reaching out to shake Supervisor Harold Statz' hand. "When do you leave?"

"I'll be leaving here the 30th. We're planning to take a week's vacation, so I'll be starting at the area office on around the 10th of next month."

Jacobs figured she had a better-than-even chance to fill his shoes. She knew the job, had a good record, and worked well with customers.

A few days later, Jacobs heard a rumor. She went straight to Statz to check it out.

"Is Pete Grupp going to be your replacement?" she asked bluntly.

"Where'd you hear that?" he replied. Her question had taken him by surprise.

"I know you don't like to be pushed, Hal, but I honestly thought I had a good chance for the job."

"Ros, you know I'm no chauvinist. My wife's got her own career—the whole bit. But I think I can prove to you this is one job that *must* be done by a man."

"What do you mean?"

"I mean that maybe things will change someday, but right now every one of our customers is a man. The person who takes this job will have to do a lot of entertaining—drinks, dinners, an occasional night on the town—and while you may be perfectly happy to invite the customers out, I don't think they'd accept."

"Why not? They all know me. I've worked with all of them at one time or other over the last few years."

"It doesn't matter how well they know you or how much they like you."

"I don't understand."

"Yes you do. Even if they wanted to accept your invitation, I don't think their wives would be very happy about the idea."

"Then my husband will come along. Or I'll invite other people along. Hal, I can't believe that's all you're worried about."

"It's not all I'm worried about. You may recall that a couple of times a year I take them on weekend hunting and fishing trips and you couldn't even *ask* them to do that."

"How come you never discussed this with me before? I never thought you considered those things part of the job."

"I don't *think* they're part of the job, I *know* they are. If I give you my job when I move to the area office, it'll just mess both of us up, because you'll end up losing business. We do have competitors, you know."

"Then . . . I was never even in the running, was I?"

"Look, I'm going to be area manager starting next month, and I have even bigger things in mind for you in the area office. I'm just asking you to be a little patient."

RESULT: In a similar case, the woman filed a charge of sex discrimination and her case wound up before the EEOC. Although the company insisted that "sex (in this case, male) is a bona fide occupational qualification reasonably necessary to

Dealing with Day-to-Day Supervisory Problems

the normal operation of this particular business", the EEOC disagreed. In finding for the woman, the EEOC noted that the company's own requirements for the supervisory post included only product knowledge, knowledge of administration, and an ability to close sales. "Charging Party's personnel file indicates she was considered to be an above average employee . . . We conclude that Respondent refused to consider Charging Party for the promotion . . . because of her sex."

COMMENT: The EEOC is quite explicit about cases like these in its *Guidelines on Discrimination Because of Sex:* "The refusal to hire an individual because of the preferences of co-workers, the employer, *clients, or customers"* (emphasis added) does not "warrant the application of the bona fide occupational qualification exception". As a general rule, the EEOC has said it believes "that the BFOQ exception as to sex should be interpreted narrowly." The Commission gives two yardsticks by which to measure how well sex can be fitted to a job description: "authenticity or genuineness," and cites as examples, jobs for actors or actresses.

Business and Displeasure

For years, Karen Farre had wondered how much her looks had to do with her getting ahead in her work. In her first few jobs she'd had the uncomfortable feeling that the men who'd hired her just wanted to have her around to look at. However, in her last job a female supervisor had told her that her work was excellent and had given her two raises and a promotion.

Then, when she'd applied for her current job, the company had given her an aptitude test. They never told her the exact scores, but they did tell her she was in the "exceptional" range.

The test results, coupled with her previous success under a female supervisor, had given her real confidence in her ability.

Despite these successes, her current boss, John Grunwald, had managed to make her uneasy, by occasionally being more flirtatious than business-like. Whatever they talked about—her work, production problems, departmental routines—he always made some remark about her looks ("How come you're not in the movies?", "You notice how much faster the guys have been working since you've been here?") Sometimes his comments seemed more like probes designed to find out how "available" she was, such as remarks about her boyfriend, when he didn't know whether she had one or not. Farre had always gone out of her way not to let her personal life interfere with her work, but she knew that with Grunwald that wasn't going to be easy.

During her first weeks on the job, Farre laughed at her supervisor's remarks; she didn't want to seem like a wet blanket. Then she tried ignoring them by continuing to talk about business. But that only resulted in his making *more* wisecracks—assuming she hadn't heard the first ones.

Farre didn't know what to do. She knew it was only a matter of time before the supervisor would try to get a lot friendlier.

One Friday, Grunwald asked her out to lunch. The way he did it, Farre wasn't sure if it was a social or business invitation. In any event, she didn't feel she should refuse a first lunch invitation from her boss, so she accepted.

The following week, Grunwald asked her out to lunch again. This time, Farre politely refused. After a third invitation and refusal, Grunwald asked her out to dinner, but she declined the offer. Somehow her refusals were making him even more persistent.

Finally, what Farre regarded as the inevitable happened. The supervisor made what amounted to a thinly disguised "proposition."

"This is my job," she explained, getting up to leave his office, using as neutral and business-like a voice as she could.

Dealing with Day-to-Day Supervisory Problems

"I like it here. I like the work and I like the company. I hope you'll continue to find my work satisfactory." Farre thought she'd gotten out of the situation fairly gracefully until Grunwald made an attempt to put his arm around her. When Farre politely, but firmly, refused his advances, Grunwald became enraged.

After that, her life on the job became miserable. Grunwald began to criticize everything she did—and in a loud voice so everyone could hear. Sometimes he stood in the middle of the floor berating her, running down her work. "You know you can't get by forever on your looks!" he shouted.

Although Farre was past the point where her confidence was affected by such remarks, she knew that eveyone who'd heard would be wondering—and *that* she found humiliating.

"Miss Farre!" Grunwald snapped one morning. Everyone looked up. "May I *please* see you in my office—*if* you're not too *busy*."

When she was seated in his office he got right to the point. "I won't mince words, Karen. Your work has been going downhill for some time."

"In what way?" Farre inquired, keeping her poise.

"In every way. It just stinks. It's crappy, inferior work."

Farre saw how angry he was and she knew it had nothing to do with her work.

"There may be things I haven't done exactly right from time to time," she said evenly, "but it doesn't seem to me it's that bad. Could you please tell me where you think I've fallen short?"

"I really can't spend any more time on this, Karen. I have work to do. We're going to have to let you go."

RESULT: In a similar case, the woman filed a complaint, claiming her dismissal was based on sex discrimination. She claimed she'd been fired because she'd refused her supervisor's sexual advances and that the firing violated Title VII. The case ended up in court, where her former supervisor insisted that she was fired for good cause: poor performance. The court, however, decided in favor of the complainant, finding the discharge retaliatory in violation of Title VII as the woman had contended. The supervisor's behavior, the court observed, had established an "artificial barrier to employment which was placed before one gender and not the other. . . . There can be no question that the prohibition against sex discrimination reaches all discrimination affecting employment which is based on gender." In other words, the demands made on the female employee were not made on male employees. And when demands are made only on employees of one sex, it constitutes sex discrimination. (The case is being appealed.)

COMMENT: More and more women are taking strong stands against social—or sexual—coercion on the job. Complaints have been filed because of insulting or demeaning remarks and physical advances. While this area of sex discrimination has still not been clearly defined by the EEOC or the courts, it's likely that some protection will be extended to women to protect them against being physically taken advantage of, or simply being mistreated in the workplace. Without such protection, female employees' personal and economic rights could potentially be abridged either by male co-workers or by male superiors (supervisors, managers, executives) who hold over them the power of economic survival.

RACE AND NATIONAL ORIGIN DISCRIMINATION

Supervisors often decide that since certain employees look or talk differently, they should be treated differently. That's where most problems begin. Try to put aside your assumptions about the minority group to which the employee belongs and deal with her or him as an individual. Avoid the temptation to deal with all members of a minority group through a representative.

Apply the same standards to all employees. You can cause as much trouble and resentment by overcompensating and treating minority employees with "kid gloves" as you can by discriminating against them. Make an honest effort to help employees do their job well, but don't praise poor work simply to avoid conflict.

Don't immediately assume that someone with an accent shouldn't be dealing with the public. If you think that perfect diction is a "business necessity," be prepared to prove it. Remember that if it doesn't interfere with the job, people at work can speak among themselves in any language they wish.

Employee or customer preference (real or imagined) should not affect hiring and job assignment decisions with regard to Black or foreign-born employees.

Bad Business Sense

Monday morning, Lloyd Morgan and two other trainees reported to the Western District Sales Office. The fact that he was the only black sales person out of twenty in the department was not lost on Morgan.

The morning began with a sales meeting—actually, it was more of a pep-talk than a meeting—then the group broke up. Morgan and the other two trainees watched them all file out with their sample cases while the three waited for Sales Supervisor Jerry Marsalis to assign them to their territories.

Marsalis assigned the first two salesmen to the Northern and Eastern Districts, respectively.

"Lloyd," the supervisor continued, "I'd like you to take the Central District. We haven't had a regular rep there in a while, so it should be good pickings."

Morgan was familiar enough with the area to know that it was solidly black—and poor.

However, he decided to say nothing about it until he'd given it a try. That way, if he wanted to change territories he'd at least have a track record.

Morgan did well his first few months. That is, he thought he was doing well until he began to compare notes with the other salespeople and discovered that he was averaging around 25 percent less than everybody else. And he wasn't going on any fish stories; he could verify what the others had said simply by checking Marsalis' weekly sales charts on the bulletin board.

Morgan redoubled his efforts. He started a little earlier in the morning, worked through his lunch hours, and stayed,on the job overtime. He even began putting in time Saturday mornings.

But it did no good. Not only did his sales fail to increase—they began to go down.

"Say, I was wondering what's involved in changing territories?" Morgan inquired, after a Monday morning sales meeting.

"You having problems?" Marsalis replied.

"I guess you might say that. I'm averaging about 25 percent less than everyone else."

"Well, let's go over your approach. What's your pitch?"

"Hold it, hold it," Morgan said. "There's nothing wrong with my pitch. I outdid everybody my first few weeks."

Dealing with Day-to-Day Supervisory Problems

"It's not unusual for people to start off with a bang and then hit a dry spell. Selling is like that."

"But I never had any dry spell. Let's face it, Jerry, the stores in the black area just haven't got a lot of money. I could work 24 hours a day, seven days a week in that district and it wouldn't do any good. If they're not doing the business, they haven't got the bread, and if they haven't got the bread, I'm just wasting my time."

"Well, what do you want me to do?"

"I'd like you to give me another territory."

"But you were hired specifically to sell in the Central District."

"Nobody ever told me that."

"It makes good business sense, doesn't it?"

"Not to me."

RESULT: In a similar case, the employee filed a complaint with the EEOC, which made the following ruling: "Charging Party, a salesman, alleged that employer assigned him to 'all Negro accounts' because of his race and that such accounts netted less revenue than those assigned to similarly placed white employees.... It is apparent that Charging Party would not have been assigned 'all Negro' accounts but for his race. Accordingly, we conclude that such a disparate and racially based work assignment constitutes an unlawful employment practice under Title VII...." The EEOC also found the hiring policy to be discriminatory, concluding that since there was only one Negro district, "Negroes were excluded from consideration for any but the position for which Charging Party was hired. Such practices are unlawful."

COMMENT: Supervisors know that on the one hand, their EEO responsibilities require that they give every individual a chance to be hired, trained and promoted without respect to race, color, religion, etc., and that on the other, they have an affirmative responsibility to see to it that these efforts are not token—that women and minorities have some kind of proportional representation in the better paying, higher level jobs. But neither of these responsibilities should be construed to mean that blacks should be matched with blacks, women with women, etc., either within a department or in establishing liaisons with other departments, companies, or customers. To do so would be to violate the spirit and letter of EEO law, because such action is based on the assumption that being black or female overrides personality differences, as well as individual differences in intelligence, skill, experience, education, and other factors. In the case described above, even if the Negro district had netted the Negro salesman the same amount as a white district would have, assigning him to the territory would still have been discriminatory because the assignment would have been based on the employee's race. And employment decisions based on race, sex, etc., are in violation of Title VII.

The Quiet One

Supervisor Tom Krystak needed a new typesetter in a hurry for two reasons. First, his other typesetter had left on only two days notice and Krystak simply couldn't run his department for more than a few days without a replacement. Second, Krystak thought he might be leaving the company, himself, soon and he wanted to make sure he left his department in good order.

One of the first resumes he saw was from Hector Montoya, a typesetter with over 16 years experience. Krystak made an appointment to see Montoya right away, and arranged for him to take a typesetting test just to see if he was as good as his resume.

Montoya arrived punctually at 8:30 A.M. the following

Dealing with Day-to-Day Supervisory Problems

morning. As they introduced themselves, Krystak noticed that Montoya had a thick Spanish accent. This worried the supervisor until Montoya took the test. He completed it without a mistake and in less than the allotted time.

Soon after Montoya had been hired, Krystak left the firm. His replacement, Brian Herlihy, was brought in from outside. At the same time, the company got two new contracts.

Although the new supervisor's department was not directly involved in both new jobs, there was some additional work for him. Because Montoya's workload would be increasing quite a bit, Herlihy told him about the new contracts and explained what would be expected of him in the way of added work.

The typesetter kept up with the increased workload for a few weeks, but then began to fall behind. Herlihy, anxious to prove himself as the new head of the department, became uneasy. As he began to work with Montoya more closely and talk to him more frequently, the supervisor began to wonder if there was also a communication problem. For the most part he seemed to understand the typesetter, but he was never sure if Montoya understood *him*. The way Montoya looked at him and just nodded, or mumbled "yes" or "no" Herlihy was inclined to think the typesetter wasn't getting the message.

Between Herlihy's concern about his own job and his uncertainty about Montoya, he felt himself working under mounting pressure.

One morning Leadman Bernie Wyler came by.

"Is Montoya having any trouble fitting in the subheads on the index?" he asked.

"He didn't say, Bernie," Herlihy replied, frowning.

"Oh ..." Wyler hesitated. "Does that mean there isn't any trouble?"

"To be perfectly honest, Bernie, I don't know what it means. He doesn't have much to say and I can't tell when he understands me and when he doesn't. Do you ever have a problem talking to the guy?"

"Well, I don't have too much trouble understanding him, but, like you said, I'm never sure if he knows what *I'm* talking about."

"Anybody else mention if they're having a problem?"

"One or two guys. Same thing. The accent doesn't bother them, but they're never sure how Hector reads them."

"Okay, Bernie, I'll keep my ears open. He's a nice guy but if no one can talk to him, he's not much use."

The supervisor spent the rest of the morning going over layouts.

Later that afternoon, he asked his secretary if she'd had any difficulty talking to Montoya. His secretary not only said she'd had absolutely no problem, she seemed surprised by his question.

During the next week, Montoya's backlog grew. Herlihy, who was beginning to get questions from his boss about deadlines, decided he had to act. He gave Montoya a warning. He told the typesetter that his performance would have to improve—particularly in terms of weekly productivity.

Montoya, however, continued to fall behind. Herlihy gave him a second warning, and then a third. Finally, the supervisor gave Montoya his notice. His reasons: poor productivity and general difficulty with communication. He felt the typesetter had a language problem that could not be overcome.

Immediately following the discharge, two things happened: Herlihy hired two typesetters to handle the backlog and rising workload—and Montoya filed a charge of discrimination with the EEOC claiming he'd been fired because of his national origin.

RESULT: A similar case eventually wound up before the EEOC. During the investigation, the employer testified that the discharged employee was not able to perform his assigned tasks because of a "language problem." The man himself vigorously denied that he had any such problem. According to

Dealing with Day-to-Day Supervisory Problems

other testimony, however, "his supervisor, as well as his co-workers indicate that they had no problem understanding the employee but *assumed that he had problems understanding them* (emphasis added). The office secretary stated that she ... did not feel he had trouble understanding anyone...."

In the face of this conflicting testimony, the EEOC examined the typesetter's past record. He'd had two years of military service and 16 years as a typesetter. The Commission was convinced that both "required the ability to communicate in English," invalidating the employer's contention that he had a language problem.

The EEOC also pointed out that the one discharged typesetter had been replaced by *two* new employees, strongly indicating that the discharged employee had fallen behind in his workload because he'd been expected to do two jobs.

The EEOC found the employer in violation of Title VII for discharging the employee because of his national origin (Spanish-surnamed American).

COMMENT: The supervisor and the typesetter's co-workers may have *assumed* that the man had a problem understanding others because of his accent, but an assumption is obviously not a fact. When you think an employee is having trouble understanding you, check it out. Ask the individual to "play back" what you've said as he understands it—assignments rules, regulations, corrections, etc. Some managers do this with all employees as a matter of routine. It helps to close communication gaps between sender and receiver—gaps based on what the sender wants to say and what he actually says, or gaps stemming from certain words having different meanings to sender and receiver. Note that the EEOC checked the employee's past record before making a decision—a common Commission practice. Managers would be well-advised to do the same before taking any extreme disciplinary action.

Shades of Bias

Mabel Hubbel knew from experience that because she was extremely dark many white people responded to her differently than they did to blacks with lighter skin.

Nevertheless she felt confident about her forthcoming job interview. With her high school degree, the half year she'd spent at a secretarial school, and her job experience, Hubbel thought herself well-qualified.

As she pulled into the company parking lot she reviewed the things she wanted to say at the interview.

A few minutes later, she presented herself at the main desk.

Office Supervisor Howard Kurtz sat in his office checking Hubbel's resume one last time before her expected arrival. In addition to her being competent, Kurtz hoped she'd be well dressed. As a receptionist, she'd be the first person clients saw as they came in.

A moment later his intercom buzzed. Hubbel had arrived and was waiting to see him.

"Glad you could make it this morning," the supervisor said courteously as his secretary showed Hubbel in.

Kurtz was pleased to see that she was quite well dressed and neat in appearance. But he was struck by how dark she was. It reminded him how few blacks there were in the company. The truth was, of 135 employees, Kurtz wasn't sure there were any.

This fact had not been lost on Hubbel as she'd been led through the maze of desks on the way to Kurtz's office. She'd quickly realized that if she was hired—and that seemed like a bigger "if" now that she'd seen the place—she might be the only black there.

After a few introductory remarks, Kurtz began to ask questions.

"Your background looks okay, but I don't see where

Dealing with Day-to-Day Supervisory Problems 73

you've ever been a receptionist. This *is* what we're looking for, you know."

"Oh, I know. Actually I've done everything a receptionist does but in different jobs. So, even though I've never been *called* a receptionist, I am qualified.

"Like in my last job," she continued, "I was secretary to the head of personnel. I met everybody who came to the department, I had to answer the phone and take messages for my boss and for other departments nearby, and when someone called the company and wasn't sure who they wanted, the switchboard always transferred the call to me."

"Then you didn't actually handle the switchboard yourself?"

"Not in that job. But in the one before, handling the switchboard was *all* I did."

"All . . . right," said Kurtz, picking up her resume and looking at it again.

"Like I said, I've done everything a receptionist does but *be* a receptionist."

"Okay. I'd like to give you a typing test as I mentioned on the phone."

"Fine."

"Then we'll see what's what."

After Hubbel took the test, she was shown out with an assurance that she'd hear from the company within 10 days.

When, after two weeks, Hubbel had received no word, she phoned Kurtz, but could not reach him.

She left a message, but received no return call or letter.

It took Hubbel nearly four weeks to get through to someone who would give her concrete information. And the information she finally got was that the job had been filled.

Convinced that the issue was race rather than job qualifications, Hubbel filed a discrimination charge against the company, claiming she'd been denied the job because of her "race or color."

The case eventually wound up before the EEOC. But before it reached the EEOC, a state agency made an investigation.

At the same time Hubbel came across some information that greatly disturbed her. Not only was the woman who'd been hired far less qualified than she—even more frustrating, she too was black!

RESULT: In a similar case, the employer insisted that the charge was obviously false since the person who got the job was herself black. But the EEOC noted that while the successful applicant might technically be called "Negro", she was, in fact, so light in color any such classification would indeed be technical.

So the Commission sustained the discrimination charge, commenting: "The employer contends that because it hired a Negro for its receptionist position it is exonerated of discrimination. Superficially, the contention appears meritorious. However, it is rooted in the assumption that persons of the Negro race are "alike."

"The fallacy is demonstrated here by the fact that investigation disclosed that the Negro applicant selected for the receptionist position is 'extremely light-complexioned,' and of distinct 'Caucasian features,' while Charging Party is 'dark-complexioned,' with 'Negroid features.' Although Charging Party and the person hired are nearly the same age, Charging Party has considerably more work experience and education."

The EEOC also noted that the light-complexioned woman accepted for the job was the only person of her race hired by the company and concluded that "color was a factor in [the employer's] refusal to hire [the darker applicant]."

COMMENT: There are two important issues in this case. The first is that the EEOC bases its findings on the overall picture and is not interested in hair-splitting definitions, such as who is, or is not, "Negro" where blacks are clearly not receiving equal treatment. The second is that when there is a pattern of discrimination (this company has no other black employees),

Dealing with Day-to-Day Supervisory Problems

otherwise secondary or peripheral factors become primary evidence. Had blacks been well represented in the company's work force, darkness or lightness of skin color might never have been an issue.

RELIGIOUS DISCRIMINATION

Since you are not permitted to ask about a job applicant's religious beliefs during the hiring process, you may discover afterward that you've hired someone whose religious observance seems to conflict with the job requirements. At that point you must determine whether "reasonable accommodation" will allow the employee to fulfill his or her religious needs. The alternative is deciding and proving that the employee's religious observance would cause "undue hardship" to the running of your business.

For employees whose Sabbath or religious holidays conflict with work hours, try to arrange shift changes or other ways in which they can make up the lost work. Avoid making blanket policies such as "everyone has to work on Saturday." There will be cases where accommodation will be very difficult, but be aware that the Courts have a very narrow view of "undue hardship."

Be prepared to accommodate yourself to the wearing of special clothing. If you want the employee to wear clothes other than those his religion requires him to wear, make sure you can prove the necessity of your requirement. The same applies to other forms of day-to-day religious observances as well (e.g. special dietary requirements).

The Convert

Hazel Williams seemed more serious lately, more reserved. She'd cut her Afro short and had begun to wear more conserva-

Dealing with Day-to-Day Supervisory Problems

tive clothes. Only a few of her closest friends and her supervisor, Laura Schneck knew the reason: Hazel Williams had recently converted to the religion of Islam. She was studying to be a Black Muslim.

"Could I speak to you for a minute?" Williams asked her supervisor, one morning.

"Sure, Hazel. What's up?"

"Do you remember I told you that I was studying to be a Black Muslim?"

"Sure I do," Schneck replied.

"Well, in a few weeks, I'm going to have to start wearing different clothes."

"We're pretty open about dress here," Schneck said, "as long as it's not attention-getting."

"I'm afraid you might think the clothes I'll have to wear are attention-getting."

"If they are, you'll have to wear something else."

Two weeks later Williams came in wearing a long gown with long sleeves and a high neckline. Schneck immediately called her into her office.

"Hazel, I believe I told you that while my policy on dress is pretty flexible, I do have to draw the line at attention-getting outfits and I'm afraid that what you're wearing is pretty conspicuous."

"The religion of Islam requires that I wear it."

"Look, Hazel, whatever group you want to join is your business, but . . ."

"It's not a group," Williams cut in. "It's a religion."

"In any case, you can't wear that. You'll have to wear something else."

"I'm not permitted to."

"Well . . . I'm sorry. The choice is yours."

"I guess I'll have to quit then."

"It's up to you."

The next day, Williams quit.

RESULT: In a similar case, the employee later filed a complaint with the EEOC. Despite the supervisor's contention that the employee had quit voluntarily because she did not wish to comply with the company's definition of appropriate business attire, the EEOC ruled that the employee "did not voluntarily quit, but was forced to choose between the mode of dress required by her religious beliefs and continuing in [the company's] employ. We conclude that [the employee] was constructively discharged."

COMMENT: Two important issues raised by this case are:

(1) *What constitutes a religion in terms of EEOC?* Since there are many small religious sects, each with its own special practices and observances, how do you know which ones are covered by Title VII's prohibition against discrimination because of religion? The answer is that the EEOC's definition of what constitutes a religion is very broad. In commenting on this case, for example, the EEOC quoted the Supreme Court's ruling in conscientious objector cases which defined religion for legal purposes as "a sincere and meaningful belief which occupies in the life of its possessor a place parallel to that filled by the God of those admittedly qualifying for the exemption . . ." It even extended the statutory definition of religion to cover "intensely personal" convictions which many people might consider "incomprehensible" or "incorrect."

(2) *"Reasonable Accommodation."* Once it is established that an employee needs to do something for religious reasons, then, according to EEOC guidelines, employers must make "reasonable accommodation" for employees' religious observances or practices which differ from the employer's schedules, standards or other business-related conditions. The only time you don't have to make such accommodations is when an employee's religious practices or observances cause

"undue hardship" on the safe and efficient operation of the business. But the burden of proving "undue hardship" is on you.

"Everybody's Up In Arms"

As Pete Blake collected his things, he got icy stares from the rest of the people in Maintenance—and he knew why. It was only 3 p.m. and the shift wasn't scheduled to end till 4 p.m.

Blake was leaving early because it was Friday afternoon and his religion required that he not work from sundown Friday to sundown Saturday.

"Good-bye, Mr. Wiel," Blake said somewhat formally to his supervisor. "See you on Monday."

"So long, Pete," Wiel replied.

Then Wiel went out on the floor to remind those who were on the Saturday shift that they'd be working the following day.

"Al, just want to remind you, you have the Saturday shift this week, okay?"

"Yeah, I know," the man said angrily. "I'm doin' it this week, but don't depend on my workin' Saturdays forever. I might just go and get me the right kind of religion so I can have the weekends off, too—like Blake."

"You're entitled to your religious observance same as anyone else," Wiel said.

Wiel knew that there was resentment about Blake's Sabbath observance and about his being off on certain other special holidays, but as long as the grumbling remained just grumbling, Blake was conscientious enough for Wiel to be willing to make allowances for him.

A few weeks later, Wiel was transferred and a new supervisor, Ted Buckley, took over.

"I thought I should tell you," Blake explained to the new

supervisor, "that my religion does not permit me to work from sundown Friday to sundown Saturday and on certain other special holidays."

"Yes, Wiel told me about it," Buckley replied.

"I thought I should tell you myself."

"It's okay with me as long as it doesn't cause trouble," Buckley said flatly.

Unfortunately, however, while Blake's co-workers had begrudgingly accepted his religious observances under their former supervisor, they seemed unwilling to go along with it under the new supervisor, Ted Buckley. What had been occasional grumbling now became intense and widespread resentment.

"It just ain't right," one of the senior maintenance workers told Buckley one afternoon. "Everybody's up in arms about it. You better know there's gonna be some real angry folks around here if something isn't done."

Buckley called Blake in and told him about the resentment his Sabbath observance was causing.

"Look, maybe I could put in time for someone in some other way or take on some of the dirtier jobs," Blake offered. "I'll do what I can to make it fairer."

"I appreciate your attitude, but I don't think it's practical."

"I've tried to schedule as many of my vacation days as possible so they fall on my religious holidays," Blake said.

"I know you've tried. But I have a real morale problem here. The whole department is in a stew about this thing. I hate to do this, but I'm going to have to give you a choice: Either you put in your Saturdays like everyone else or I'll have to let you go."

"I simply can't do that. My faith forbids me to work on the Sabbath."

"It's your choice," Buckley said quietly. "I'm sorry. I'll have to let you go."

Bitter over his discharge, Blake filed a charge with the EEOC complaining that he'd been discriminated against because of his religion.

Dealing with Day-to-Day Supervisory Problems 81

RESULT: In a similar case, the company wound up in court. A lower court ruled in favor of the company, saying that the discharge was justified. The court notes that an employer is obligated to make "reasonable accommodation" to an employee's religious beliefs unless that reasonable accommodation results in "undue hardship" to the employer—which in this case, the court ruled, it had. The discharged employee, however, appealed to a higher court, which reversed the employee's termination. "The objections and complaints of fellow employees," said the court, "in and of themselves do not constitute 'undue hardship in the conduct of an employer's business.' " Although the court conceded that if morale were to be affected seriously enough, this could be construed as "undue hardship," it rules that in this case the company had not substantiated its undue-hardship claim.

COMMENT: When a production run, or project hits a snag, you don't simply drop it—you use your ingenuity and experience to find some way to solve the problem. Try the same approach with EEO problems. One of the factors in the higher court's deciding against the company in this case was the fact that the company hadn't made a sufficient effort to resolve employee misgivings. Could Blake have started his shift earlier and/or ended later? Could he have worked Sundays? Etc. Your responsibilities for production and for EEO enforcement have one thing in common: Problems that arise in either area must be solved—they cannot be gotten rid of.

AGE DISCRIMINATION

Recently, older employees joined the groups receiving legal protection from employment discrimination. Government regulations aside, it makes good business sense to take advantage of what the older employee has to offer.

When seeking applicants for an opening, avoid want-ad phrases such as "1 year experience," "junior staffer," "recent grad." Although usually used to indicate starting (and therefore low) salaries, they are now sometimes regarded as suggesting youth. Know that the law considers age to be a bona fide occupational qualification for very few jobs.

Don't be afraid to hire an older employee simply because your current workforce is predominantly young. This is just as unfair and unlawful as not hiring a woman into an all male department or a black into an all white group.

Never fail to give a deserved raise or promotion to an employee who has only a few years to go until retirement. Keep training programs open to all employees, regardless of age.

When taking action against an employee, don't justify that action in any way by the employee's age. When a charge is filed against your organization, it need only be shown that your decision was based in *any* way on the employee's age for the entire decision to be found unlawful.

The Hunch That Turned Into A Court Suit

With the new wing opening in a few weeks, Maintenance Supervisor Don Mackey got word that he'd be hiring a few more people for his crew.

"How many do you think we'll need?" Mackey asked the plant's superintendent.

Dealing with Day-to-Day Supervisory Problems

"I'd say at least three—let's start with three, anyway. If you need more you can borrow somebody from Shipping until we get someone else."

"Is there any particular way you want me to do this? I thought I'd put an ad in the Chronicle."

"Fine. Oh, there's one other thing," the plant superintendent said. "Most of the work in the new wing is going to be dyeing and finishing. Whoever you get is going to have to do a lot of heavy work. Those drums weigh plenty even when they're empty."

Mackey put an ad in the local paper and soon received a number of replies. He was particularly interested in a man he'd spoken to on the phone named Blair Watson. Watson said he'd had over 15 years' experience in maintenance work and that he'd also driven a truck, so he was used to lifting heavy weights.

But when Mackey saw Watson, he did a take. Mackey's reaction was not lost on Watson—he knew something was wrong and he had a pretty good idea what it was. The supervisor simply hadn't expected to see a man in his 50's applying for the job.

"As I told you on the phone," Watson said during the interview, "I had some 15 years' experience as a maintenance man for another textile plant and I worked for them as a trucker, too. So, I know how to tear down machines and lube them—and I can do the heavy work."

"Well, that kind of background is certainly very important," Mackey said, trying to sound enthusiastic. But his voice rang hollow.

When the interview was over, Watson felt pretty depressed. He had everything they wanted, but he had a strong hunch he wasn't going to get any of the three jobs.

Watson felt he'd gotten a raw deal, but he didn't know what to do about it. His wife suggested he call up someone at the local state employment office. They, in turn, suggested that he write to Employment Standards Administration in the Wages and Hours Division of the Department of Labor, which is responsible for administering the "Age Discrimination in Employment Act of 1967."

Mackey wrote a letter describing the newspaper ad, the phone conversation, and subsequent interview.

RESULT: Within a few weeks, Mackey's letter produced results. The Department of Labor sent a representative to the area and took a statement from Mackey. Because the company was in a small town, word had gotten around about other older men who'd been turned down for the same job. Their statements were taken, too. In the end, the Department of Labor decided to take the company to court. After the evidence was heard, the judge concluded that the men had been turned down for the jobs because of their age (over 50), in violation of the law.

COMMENT: If you think age is a qualification for a particular job, be prepared to prove it in court. What you must prove is that *everyone* over a certain age is incapable of doing the job, and that can be pretty difficult. Anyone who watches sports knows there are some great baseball players in their forties and some football players who have played into their fifties. Although the Labor Department tries to remedy discrimination complaints administratively before it goes to court, why not match job requirements with experience and ability instead of age and avoid getting involved with a government agency in the first place?

DISCRIMINATION AGAINST THE HANDICAPPED

The Rehabilitation Act of 1973 requires government contractors and subcontractors to take affirmative action to "employ and advance in employment qualified handicapped individuals." (A "qualified handicapped individual" is someone who fits the law's definition of handicapped given below, and who is capable of performing a particular job if *reasonable accommodation* is made to his or her handicap. This will be explained later on.) The law is fairly specific about what it expects: "The contractor agrees to take affirmative action . . . in all employment practices such as the following: employment, upgrading, demotion or transfer, recruitment, advertising, layoff or termination, rates of pay or other forms of compensation, and selection for training, including apprenticeship."

What Should You Do?

Supervisors whose organizations are government contractors (or subcontractors), or whose organizations have Affirmative Action Plans covering the handicapped for other reasons, need to know three things: What is meant by the term "handicapped," how to integrate handicapped employees into your workforce, and how to supervise them.

The Rehabilitation Act of 1973 contains guidelines in which it defines a handicapped individual as "any person who has a physical or mental impairment which substantially limits one or more of such person's major life activities [*communication, walking, self-care, socialization, education, vocational training, employment, transportation, etc.*], has a record of such impairment [*and has recovered, yet continues to be discriminated against because of the attitude of employers, supervisors and co-workers toward the person's previous impairment, particularly heart attacks, cancer, and mental illness*] or is regarded as having such an impairment."

You may be wondering what "regarded as having such an impairment" means. The phrase is designed to cover those who have no real handicaps, yet *appear to* and therefore have just as much trouble getting jobs, keeping them, or getting ahead in them as those who really are handicapped.

To sum it up, the law defines handicaps both in terms of genuine physical and mental impairments as well as in terms of any physical or mental attributes that potential or current employers might *think* are impairments. If the law did not do this, those who only appeared to have disabilities would be at a greater disadvantage than those who really did have them since they would have just as much trouble getting jobs, but would have no legal protection.

But Can They Really Do the Job?

A study conducted by E. I. duPont de Nemours & Co. (Wilmington, Delaware) revealed some interesting facts: Handicapped employees did as well as, or better than, non-handicapped employees in such areas as attendance, getting to work on time, positive work attitudes, reliability, and loyalty to the company. The extent or nature of the disability, it was discovered, bore no relation to performance. On the contrary, those with the greatest handicaps did best. When company supervisors evaluated the 1,500 handicapped workers on safety, on-the-job performance, and turnover, they found that over 90% rated average or better than average in all three categories.

Get the Facts—And Use Them

Before assigning jobs or tasks to handicapped employees, *ask* them if they have any limitations. You'll get a straight answer. Chances are, they'll tell you that their limitations won't affect the jobs they're applying for (or have been hired for). If you think they have limitations they haven't mentioned, or if you can't see how they're going to be able to do the job with the limitations they have discussed ask them about this—and be honest and straightforward about it.

When just talking about possible work problems doesn't alleviate your doubts, try to find out from Personnel what restrictions the doctor thinks are necessary. In cases where handicapped employees have not taken a physical, the organization which is hiring them may request an examination—and, of course, must pay for it.

But whether you find out about a physical or mental impairment from the handicapped employee himself, or from the results of the physical, *take no action* unless the impairment is job related.

When handicapped employees enter your department, use the same criteria for placing them in jobs that you would for non-handicapped workers: individual physical and mental abilities, experience, training, temperament, etc. For example, even though you would not normally assign frail people to heavy work, or abrasive individuals to work with people, you might use both employees in areas where they had strengths. Extend the same thoughtfulness, the same managerial skill and knowledge to handicapped employees.

Should you need more help than your organization can offer in finding the right job (or tasks) for handicapped employees, there are a number of nationwide government agencies which can assist you in placing handicapped workers in the right kinds of jobs (and help you to recruit and train them, too). The U.S. Employment Service, the Veterans Administration, and the Office of Vocational Rehabilitation are three of the best known. Local hospitals and rehabilitation centers are also good sources, as are sheltered workshops.

Our Crowd

Use your ingenuity in integrating handicapped employees into your work force both with the work itself and socially. See if their abilities can be used in combination with those of other handicapped or non-handicapped employees.

At the same time, remind non-handicapped workers that although others may not be able to see, hear, or move as they can, they still have the same feelings—emotional and sexual—the desire for acceptance and ambition to get ahead, the same hope and expectation of finding people at work they can be friendly with and talk to. Urge current employees to include the handicapped in coffee breaks and in any social activities. If the first invitations are refused it may be because handicapped workers are anxious about how well they're going to be accepted, so, please, encourage employees to be patient.

A Day's Work for a Day's Pay

Make it clear to handicapped and non-handicapped alike, that all workers in your department have the same requirements for productivity, attendance, etc., that the law does not require organizations to hire or keep people if they don't meet work standards, regardless of disability. Emphasize the fact that everyone will compete for advancement on an equal basis.

Dealing with Day-to-Day Supervisory Problems   89

Stressing equal standards will assure current employees that handicapped co-workers won't be getting the same pay for less work and it will demonstrate your respect for handicapped employees by showing that you think they're capable of doing the job.

Accommodation

The Rehabilitation Act of 1973 requires organizations (and their representatives, such as supervisors, managers, etc.) covered by the law to "make a reasonable accommodation to the physical and mental limitation of an employee or applicant" unless it can be demonstrated that "such an accommodation would impose an undue hardship on the conduct of the contractor's business." How far you must go or when you can refuse to make adjustments in accommodating employees' disabilities depends on a number of vaguely defined factors such as "business necessity" and "financial cost and expenses."

In terms of day-to-day work, one way in which you can accommodate the needs of handicapped workers is to devise new ways of doing current jobs—or simply rearranging the order in which the job is done—providing special tools or equipment, or making modifications in the work area. For example, shelves might be lowered or moved nearer for a paraplegic, light signals might be substituted for sound signals for deaf workers, labels that could be felt rather than just read might be used for blind employees to identify files, bins, etc.

It's particularly important to extend these accommodations to handicapped employees during the probationary period when their performance will determine whether or not they get the job.

Know Your State Laws

In addition to observing the Federal Act, be aware of state laws covering discrimination against the handicapped. More and more states are implementing such laws and each state's statutes vary from the next. For example, California specifically prohibits discrimination against recovered cancer victims or people who have "impairment of physical ability because of amputation, loss of function or coordination, or any other health impairment which requires special education or related services."

REVERSE DISCRIMINATION

Fear of lawsuits and overzealous affirmative action efforts have brought about charges of discrimination by a new group—white males. Supervisors sometimes forget that decisions based on race or sex that work to the disadvantage of *any* group violate the law.

While you are encouraged to seek out minority and female applicants for a job opening, it is important to make the final hiring decision based on the job requirements and the merits of *all* the applicants.

On the job, it is important to evelute all employees working in the same capacity with equal standards. Avoid the tendency to expect more from white, male employees than you do from others. Similarly there must be a uniform disciplinary approach to comparable infractions for all employees.

Don't assume that white males have too much pride to be considered for lower level jobs. They should be offered the same opportunity to get those jobs as minorities and women and judged on the same criteria. Don't decide for a job applicant that he or she is overqualified for a job.

A Fine Line

"Staff meeting," Warehouse Supervisor Sel Grofay said abruptly as he walked past his assistant, Fay Healy.

Healy was amused. As his only assistant ("My leadman is a woman," Grofay liked to say) she was the only member of his "staff." So a staff meeting was simply the two of them talking in his office.

"How are Beryl and Cindy doing?" he asked, referring to two recently hired loaders.

"They're making it." Healy replied.

"More power to 'em," said the supervisor, nodding. Five years earlier, Grofay would have laughed at the idea of hiring women as loaders. Now he actively sought them out. For the moment, though, he only had two in his warehouse doing loading work.

"What's happening with the checkers?" he continued.

"We have an opening as of the 1st. Tandy is leaving."

"Did you post it?"

"This morning. I already got some action: Tommy Bull."

"The big guy? The loader?"

"That's him."

"Did you tell him my policy?"

"I told him that since only a few women have the strength to be loaders, we save the checker spots for them—and for disabled guys."

"Good. Then there was no problem?"

"I'm afraid there was. He seemed to think that was discrimination."

"Discrimination! Oh, never mind. I'll talk to him myself."

By the time Grofay saw Bull, the loader was pretty steamed up. "I've got a good record here and I know I can do checker work. Now Healy comes along with some cock-eyed story that I have to be a woman. I don't get it."

"You should. You know this company is big on equal employment. That means we have to actively look for people who aren't already represented in our departments. You follow me?"

"So far."

"Okay. I don't have to tell you that there aren't a lot of women around who can do loading work. So far I've only found two. So, to make things a little more fair, I save the lighter work for them—and for disabled guys. I'm just trying to give everyone a fair shake."

"What about me? I'm not getting a fair shake."

Dealing with Day-to-Day Supervisory Problems

"Come on, Tom. You make good pay as a loader. Plus you get overtime. The checkers almost never do overtime."

"It all evens out in the end, Sel." Bull replied. "Anyway, that's a choice *I* should be allowed to make. If I want a job where I use my brains, you have no right to say I can't even *apply* just because I happen to be strong."

"You can apply."

"Come off it, Grofay. I'm leveling with you. Don't pull technicalities on me."

"It's not a technicality. It's my policy."

"Call it what you want. As far as I'm concerned, it's just plain discrimination."

RESULT: In a similar case, the white male employee filed a charge of discrimination with the EEOC, complaining that he'd been discriminated against because of sex (male). The supervisor denied that he'd discriminated, explaining his policy of reserving the lighter checkers' jobs for women and disabled men, since he'd found few women who could qualify for the heavier work involved in loading. The Commission acknowledged the supervisor's good intentions, agreeing that he'd "acted with honest purposes" to carry out his affirmative responsibilities in accordance with EEO law. But the EEOC saw a serious problem in the supervisor's actions. Despite his good intentions, he had gone beyond just carrying out affirmative action—filling more positions with women—and had actually established "separate employment classifications." In other words, he had segregated jobs by sex (and physical handicap). By refusing to hire (or even consider) a non-disabled, physically strong male for the checker position, he was in effect making sex (female) and physical handicap a *bona fide occupational qualification* (BFOQ). In order to make sex a BFOQ— or a requirement for the job—the employer must be prepared to prove that it is necessary to the "safe and efficient performance" of the job. And, according to EEOC guidelines, the only times it can ever be found necessary is for "authenticity or genuineness"—e.g., using women to model women's clothes or act the role of women characters, or using men similarly.

COMMENT: As complex as it may seem, the point the EEOC made in this case is really fairly simple: Don't let legitimate affirmative action become so rigid that it results in re-segregated job categories. Creating a new, segregated job classification or line of progression is just as discriminatory—and therefore unlawful—as maintaining an old one.

Humble Pie is Better Than None

At 45, Kevin Dougherty was the oldest underwriter in his department.

His job, deciding whether a particular business was worth insuring, had long since lost its challenge. He had, however, continued to do his work well despite the monotony.

But no matter how hard he applied himself, no matter how often people with less experience came to him for advice, he felt isolated. All his co-workers were younger than he. His peers had gone on to bigger and better things. Two of his former friends had become executives at other companies, several others had become supervisors in other branches of his firm, still others had gone on to do well in completely different lines of work.

Dougherty had just begun to enjoy the security of having a regular job and a steady income when the recession hit.

Small businesses began folding right and left. An avalanche of claims provoked the company to enforce more

Dealing with Day-to-Day Supervisory Problems

stringent requirements for new businesses applying for insurance.

At the same time, poor business conditions resulted in a sharp decrease in the number of people starting new businesses or seeking insurance.

It all added up to very little work for underwriters.

The word around the company was that while none of the departments were in as much trouble as the underwriters, the best anyone else was doing was holding his own.

The one exception was Auditing. Somehow it had remained unaffected by the downturn. In fact, rumor had it, Auditing still had some openings from time to time.

Actually, for the last year or so, Auditing Supervisor Pete Ostrowski had been taking on trainees—mostly women. He had been trying to get a more representative mix in what had been an all-male workforce.

Between the professional sounding title of "auditor" and the semi-skilled nature of the work, the auditing jobs provided an ideal opportunity to upgrade some of the vast numbers of women in the company's entry level secretarial, typing, and file-clerk positions.

Despite a puffy job description, an auditor's job was very routine. It consisted of linking up the right premium with the particular risks of the business to be insured. Strict company guidelines left very little room for any real decision making by the auditor.

The $7,500 starting salary for auditor-trainee was an indication of the level of skill required.

Ostrowski knew as well as anyone that the underwriters' days were numbered. He tried to think of what he might be able to do for some of them, but it was a well established practice in his department to promote from within.

That meant anyone coming in had to start as a trainee—at $7,500. The Audit Department supervisor didn't see how he could offer an underwriter who made as much as $12,500, a job that would mean a $5,000 salary cut.

Business conditions continued to worsen over the next few weeks.

Finally, the inevitable happened. One entire unit of underwriters was laid off. Kevin Dougherty was one of them.

A few days after Dougherty got his notice, an auditor-trainee spot opened in Ostrowski's unit.

The supervisor thought of offering the spot to Dougherty—the most senior underwriter and therefore the one who should get the offer—but two things stopped him.

First, he felt sure Dougherty would refuse. The $5,000 salary cut and "trainee" status at Dougherty's stage of the game—Dougherty had too much pride.

Something else bothered Ostrowski. The thought of having a man older than he in the training program made the supervisor cringe.

So, he filled the opening with a young woman from the steno pool.

By the time word of the auditor-trainee opening and the junior employee chosen to fill it had reached Dougherty, he'd been out of work for a week.

Enraged, he filed charges with every agency he could think of: a sex discrimination charge with the EEOC, an age complaint with the Wage & Hours Division of the Department of Labor, and both sex and age complaints with state and local fair employment practices agencies.

RESULT: In a similar case, the complaint was conciliated by a state agency. The company was asked to take the man back since he was more than qualified for the junior position which he had never been offered.

The company agreed to take him back. The man was rehired as an auditor-trainee.

Dealing with Day-to-Day Supervisory Problems

COMMENT: This case illustrates the kind of stereotyping that affects white males, particularly older white males. Just as women and minority employees are discriminated against because of the notion that "they don't have what it takes" to be managers, white males are sometimes not offered lower level jobs because it is assumed they have "too much pride." The end result for any group so stereotyped is frequently unemployment. Never assume that a white male employee (or anyone else) would be embarrassed, humiliated, or ashamed to be offered a cut in pay or a lower status job if that is the only alternative to termination. Always make the offer. The hard facts are that in today's economy, few people would opt for unemployment over *any* steady job.

Part Three

The following section includes useful, general information for dealing with EEO questions. It includes an outline of the federal laws currently in effect, EEO guidelines for part-time and temporary employees, and a glossary of EEO terms.

FEDERAL LAWS AGAINST DISCRIMINATION AND HOW THEY WORK

SUBJECT	Title VII of the Civil Rights Act of 1964 as amended by the Equal Employment Opportunity Act of 1972.	Executive Order 11246 as amended by E. O. 11375	Equal Pay Act of 1963	Age Discrimination In Employment Act of 1967 as amended May 1, 1974	Section 503 of the Rehabilitation Act of 1973
EMPLOYERS COVERED	Employers with 15 or more employees. Covers federal, state, local governments.	Employers holding federal contracts or subcontracts of $10,000 or more. Some branches of state or local govt.	Nearly all employers. Covers federal, state, local governments.	Any employer with 20 or more employees who work 20 or more calendar weeks in a calendar year. Covers most federal, state, local governments.	All employers with federal contracts or subcontracts of $2,500 or more. Section 501 covers federal government. State and local governments not covered.
REQUIREMENTS	That neither the employer nor his representatives —i.e., managers, supervisors, etc.—discriminate in selection, promotion, compensation, fringe benefits, training, or other conditions of employment based on race, sex, color, religion, national origin.		That there be no discrimination in salary and most fringe benefits.	That neither employer nor employer's representatives "fail or refuse to hire or to discharge any individual or otherwise discriminate with respect to his compensation, terms, conditions, or privileges of employment because of such individual's age." (Covers those 40-65 years old. State laws vary on both upper and lower age limits.)	That government contractors and subcontractors take affirmative action to employ and advance in employment qualified handicapped individuals. That neither government contractors, subcontractors nor their representatives discriminate against individuals because of their physical or mental handicap in any employment practice (hiring, training, compensation, upgrading, etc.).
ENFORCEMENT AGENCIES	Equal Employment Opportunity Commission (EEOC) for private sector. Civil Service Commission for federal employees, Justice Dept. for state and local government employees.	Office of Federal Contract Compliance Programs (OFCCP) oversees anti-discrimination programs of other agencies.	The Labor Department's Wage & Hour Division. For state and local govt. employees. Labor Dept. currently takes non-enforcement position pending clarification.	Labor Department's Wage & Hour Div. for private sector, state, and local government employees. Civil Service Commission for federal government employees.	Office of Federal Contract Compliance Programs (OFCCP) of Department of Labor.

	Title VII (EEOC)	Executive Order (OFCCP)	Equal Pay Act	Age Discrimination Act	Section 503 (Handicapped)
ENFORCEMENT POWERS	If efforts to conciliate a complaint do not succeed, the EEOC or U.S. Attorney General can file suit, as can the complainant. Court can issue injunction against further discrimination to employer, award backpay, reinstatement, etc. to complainant.	Government can cancel contracts, delay awarding of contracts, disqualify employer from future contracts.	If employer does not comply voluntarily, complainant can sue, or Sec'y of Labor can sue on complainant's behalf. Court can order reinstatement with backpay, interest, raises, etc.	An individual who wants to sue must inform the Secretary of Labor of intent to sue within 180 days of the alleged violation. Defendant would then be notified and Wage & Hour people would attempt to resolve the charge by informal methods of conciliation.	Debarment from right to bid on contracts. Withholding of progress payments. Termination or suspension of existing contracts. Filing suit in court to compel compliance under contract to rehire, promote, etc.
METHOD OF FILING COMPLAINTS	On sworn complaint form available from EEOC.	By letter to OFCCP.	In person, by letter or phone to branch of Wage & Hour office.	By phone or letter to local Wage & Hour Division.	By letter (or obtained form) to local office of Labor Dept.'s Employment Standards Administration.
WHO CAN FILE COMPLAINTS	Individuals on their own behalf or organizations on behalf of aggrieved individuals. In case of the EEOC, members of the commission may also file charges.			Individual, or representatives and organizations on behalf of individual. But investigators always talk to individual first.	Individual or representative—e.g., labor unions, friends or relatives, various organizations representing the handicapped, etc.
INVESTIGATIONS WITHOUT COMPLAINTS	No. A complaint must be filed for there to be an investigation.	Investigation can be made without complaint being filed.	Random investigations can be made.	Possible. Random investigations are very possible.	Yes, if a problem is called to OFCCP's attention.
RECORDS	Employer is required to keep and preserve all relevant records. Government is empowered to review all relevant records.	Government can review all relevant records.	Government can review records. However, how long different kinds of records must be kept varies according to Labor Dept. regulations.		Government primarily interested in records of actions taken in hiring and promotion of known handicapped individuals—if passed over, why? Where recruited? Etc.

SUBJECT	Title VII of the Civil Rights Act of 1964 as amended by the Equal Employment Opportunity Act of 1972.	Executive Order 11246 as amended by E. O. 11375	Equal Pay Act of 1963	Age Discrimination In Employment Act of 1967 as amended May 1, 1974	Section 503 of the Rehabilitation Act of 1973
INTIMIDATION OR HARASSMENT	It is unlawful for employers or their representatives—supervisors, managers, etc.—to intimidate, discipline, discharge, or otherwise harass any individual because he/she has filed a complaint, instituted proceedings, assisted in an investigation, or formally or informally objected to discriminatory practices, regardless of whether the charges or objections are valid or invalid.			It is unlawful for employers or their representatives —supervisors, managers, etc.—to intimidate, discipline, discharge or otherwise harass any individual because he/she has filed a complaint, instituted proceedings, assisted in an investigation, or formally or informally objected to discriminatory practices regardless of whether the charges or objections are valid or invalid	
CONFIDENTIALITY	Individual complainant's name is revealed to employer when the investigation begins. Although neither the EEOC nor its employees can make charges or names public, the complainant and respondent are *not* bound by this confidentiality requirement. If the case goes to court, identity of parties becomes part of the public record.	The OFCCP keeps names of parties involved confidential, but neither the complainant nor the respondent is bound by confidentiality requirement. If case goes to court, names of parties become part of public record.	Although Wage & Hour Division keeps names of parties involved confidential, neither complainant nor respondent is bound by confidentiality requirement. If case goes to court, names of parties become part of public record.	The name of the complainant is not revealed without the complainant's written permission. Charges are not made public unless the case goes to court, at which point the identities of the parties become part of the public record.	No requirements for confidentiality. Under the regulations of the Federal Privacy Act, an employee's personal record can not be made public, but there is no protection for the employer. The name of the individual filing the complaint may be given to the employer. Charges are not made public by the OFCCP.

> **NOTE:**
> - Some changes in some federal anti-discrimination laws have been proposed. These changes would primarily affect how big a contract, subcontract, or workforce should be in order to be covered by the different laws. Should they become law, *The EEO Review* will report their enactment and how they affect supervisors and other managers.
> - Remember that your state and local laws may differ in coverage or procedure from federal laws.

FEDERAL EEO LAWS: COVERAGE VARIES FOR PART-TIMERS AND TEMPORARIES

Both part-time and temporary employees receive the same coverage from Title VII and the Age Discrimination In Employment Act as full-time employees: Protection against discrimination in selection, promotion, compensation, fringe benefits, training, or other terms and conditions of employment based on race, sex, color, religion, national origin, or age.

So hiring only men for part-time (or temporary) physical work runs the same risks of violating the law as hiring only men for full-time employment.

Similarly, hiring "kids" for seasonal or part-time jobs may put a manager or his organization in violation of the age discrimination law, since older people are entitled to these jobs too.

Dollars and Cents

The Equal Pay Act of 1963 applies *only* where there is a disparity in wages for substantially equal work done by male and female employees, or where, despite a disparity in the work done, the same wages are paid men and women. It does *not* cover inequalities in compensation based on race, color, religion, national origin, or age—all of which are covered by other laws.

In fact, in enforcing the Equal Pay Act, the Labor Department's Wage and Hour Division (W & H) *cannot* get involved in pay disparities *unless* there is sex discrimination. What you want to pay your part-time or temporary employees is strictly a free market decision. Whether you want to pay them more or less than full-timers, include or exclude fringe benefits, is between your organization and its job applicants and employees—as long as males and females are adequately represented—which is decided on a case-by-case basis—and provided that male and female employees within the part-time and temporary workforce receive the same compensation for doing substantially equal work.

These are the general guidelines for enforcement of the Equal Pay Act.

As a rule of thumb, W & H defines part-time employees as those working 20 hours a week or less. Those working over 20 hours are usually considered full-time.

However, this definition is for convenience and W & H stresses that the 20-hour figure should be regarded as a general guideline and not a "magic number."

In the past, some organizations have tried to hire women for 38 or 39 hours a week to squeeze them into part-time status, saving money on both salary and fringe benefits.

So now, when W & H suspects that technicalities are being used to avoid proper compensation of female part-timers or temporaries, they investigate, and compare the full- and part-time groups to see if they're receiving equal wages and fringes.

Although W & H usually considers fringe benefits for part-time employees strictly the employer's prerogative, if the part-time workforce is all or predominantly female, the lack of fringe benefits suddenly seems based not so much on status (part-time) as on sex (female).

Never try to use "technicalities" to avoid being covered by the Equal Pay Act, either in setting hours for part-timers or in hiring practices.

For example, if you're paying a predominantly female part-time work force lower hourly wage-rates than full-time males doing the same work, you may well get in trouble with W & H. Throwing in a few male part-timers at the lower rates will not help. Only when men and women are both well represented

Dealing with Day-to-Day Supervisory Problems

in the part-time work force (and receive equal pay for equal work) does an organization "exempt" itself from W & H action under the Equal Pay Act.

Coverage for temporary employees is slightly different. The distinction is that it *is* lawful to hire an all female temporary work force and to pay them lower rates than the male (or mixed) full-time work force—provided certain conditions are met. These are:

- That the pay differential be related to the duration of the job, which must be 30 days or less.

- That the lower wage for the temporary work force be in line with the prevailing pay practices for temporary work in your industry and your company.

- That the temporary employee hired at the lower rate not be used to do higher level or more skilled work than that which they are hired to do.

As with part-time workers, the "temporary" status cannot be based on technicalities.

That means when any all, or predominantly, female temporary group is kept for more than one month, or is rehired frequently over the course of a year, W & H will begin to make comparisons between them and your full-time employees. And W & H will no longer accept the temporary status as a legitimate reason for the pay differential.

Instead, they'll take the position that a group of female temporary employees retained for more than 30 days (or repeatedly rehired) is, in fact, no longer temporary, making the previously acceptable lower wage rates unacceptable and discriminatory.

Hiring the Handicapped

In contrast to the other EEO laws, enforcers of Section 503 of the Rehabilitation Act of 1973 looks favorably upon part-time and temporary employment of handicapped individuals. While the law protects handicapped part-timers and temporaries in the same way it covers full-time handicapped employees, the OFCCP regards hiring the handicapped for part-time and temporary work as one form of *active* accommodation, since some handicapped people would prefer part-time or temporary work to full-time work because of their mental or physical disabilities.

Naturally, this should not be construed as approval or partial employment for handicapped individuals capable of doing full-time work and who are seeking full-time employment.

Executive Order 11246

Coverage of employers with federal contracts or subcontracts of $10,000 or more applies to part-time and temporary employees just as it does full-time workers.

Contractors and subcontractors must establish the same kinds of goals and timetables for adequate utilization of women and minorities in part-time and temporary work as for those in full-time positions.

State and Local Statutes

As irksome as it may be, if you hire large numbers of part-time or temporary employees, it's important to know if your state or local laws have narrower coverage. A call to your personnel department or state employment office should give you the information you need.

A GLOSSARY OF EEO TERMS

The definitions in this glossary are given in non-technical language and are designed to give a quick grasp of any terms or phrases you may come across in business or government EEO publications.

Accommodation to Handicaps. Your obligation, if your organization does business with the government, to make a reasonable accommodation to an applicant's or employee's physical and mental limitations. It may mean changing a job slightly, doing it in a different order, modifying equipment, moving supplies nearer to a workbench, etc. *Exception:* If the accommodation clearly affects the safe and efficient running of your organization or substantially affects costs, you may not have to make the accommodation.

ADEA. Stands for Age Discrimination in Employment Act of 1967.

Adverse Impact. See Disparate Effect.

Affected Class. Any group of people—blacks, women, Hispanics, etc.—which has been discriminated against or is now discriminated against in employment opportunity.

Affirmative Action Plan (AAP). An active program, with specific "goals and timetables," that gives minorities and women the opportunities in hiring, promotion, and other areas that they have missed in the past because of an organization's discriminatory policies. Government agencies and the courts judge AAP's by their *actual* results, not simply their *intended* results.

Applicant Flow Record. A written record that gives a breakdown of job applicants—how many were black, Hispanic, female, etc. It helps to show how effective an organization or department is in attracting minority and female job applicants, what percentage of these applicants are getting the jobs with the company, what percentage are not, and *why* they are not—whether they are turning down offers or are failing to qualify.

Artificial (Arbitrary or Unnecessary) Barriers to Employment. These are non-job-related requirements for employment that prevent whole groups—minorities, women, etc.—from being hired or promoted, and are therefore illegal. They may be used in recruitment, selection, placement, testing, transfers, promotion, seniority, lines of progression, or other "terms and conditions" of employment. Typical artificial barriers to employment that have been found illegal are height requirements which unfairly bar many women and Hispanics, requirements for high school diplomas which have no real relation to the skills required by *any* job and tend to screen out women or those from disadvantaged areas (usually black), and language requirements for jobs which require no real verbal communication.

Availability. A technical term that refers to the percentage of women and minorities in your company's geographic hiring area. A government agency investigating a discrimination charge or reviewing the results of an Affirmative Action Plan may compare the availability of minorities and women in your company's geographic hiring area to their percentage representation in your department to see if they are being "under-utilized" (See Underutilization).

Bona Fide Occupational Qualification (BFOQ). If you want to hire a man, someone under 40, or an applicant who speaks English without an accent, then be prepared to *prove* that the qualification you want is legitimate (bona fide). In order to prove that a sex, age, language requirement, etc., is necessary to perform the job, you have to prove that *no* woman, *no* person over 40, or *no* person with a foreign accent could do the work satisfactorily. The only BFOQ's that have made it through the courts are requirements for women to model women's clothes or play women's roles in plays and movies, or for men to do similar work. You may also specify children (age requirement) for modeling children's clothes, etc. The courts have also permitted age requirements on some jobs involving public safety such as airline pilots. Race is never a BFOQ.

Business Necessity. You may discriminate if you can *prove* that it is "essential" to the safe and efficient running of your operation, *and* that no other less discriminatory practice would work. Virtually airtight proof is required. While exceptional financial hardship sometimes qualifies as a business necessity, this too is limited. Financial losses due to real or imagined customer or employee preference *never* qualify as a business necessity. (See Customer Preference, Co-Worker Preference.)

Charging Party. The person who files a discrimination charge with the EEOC.

Chilling Effect. Questions that appear to be harmless, but in reality tend to discourage certain groups from seeking employment are said to have a chilling effect on that group and are considered discriminatory. *Example:* Asking black applicants in a ghetto area for credit references would tend to discourage all blacks in that area from even applying for a job. *Or:* A hostile working environment that results in minorities and women resigning and discourages others from applying is also said to have a chilling effect.

Class Action Suit. A law suit filed by a government agency for *all* the women (or blacks, Hispanics, etc.) in

Dealing with Day-to-Day Supervisory Problems

an organization rather than for just an individual. When the EEOC wins a class action suit, the company usually has to give back pay to members of the group(s) that were discriminated against, guarantee that more will be hired, promoted, etc., and install an Affirmative Action Plan to insure short- and long-term results.

Compliance. The degree to which an organization achieves results with its Affirmative Action Plan.

Compliance Agency. This can refer to any federal, state, or local government agency that is responsible for enforcing EEO laws, or reviewing the effectiveness of an Affirmative Action Plan.

Conciliation. Once the EEOC decides that a charge of discrimination is valid, it will try to end the discrimination by talking to the employer about it. If a whole group was discriminated against, rather than just an individual, the EEOC will ask the organization to eliminate the unfair practice(s) throughout the company. When this talking (or conciliation) fails, the EEOC sometimes takes the employer to court.

Co-Worker Preference. If your current employees, no matter how capable, don't want to work with a woman, black, Hispanic, etc., it is *not* a legal excuse for not hiring, promoting, or assigning minorities or women to any job or task.

Customer Preference. This is never an acceptable reason or "business necessity" for not observing EEO law. Even if you do all your business with one customer and that customer threatens to drop you if you hire minorities or women, it is still illegal for you to give in to the threat and discriminate. You are not permitted to defer to a customer preference which forces you to ignore a law (Title VII, the Age Discrimination Act, etc.) passed by Congress.

Disclaimer. In EEO, a disclaimer is the phrase used in want ads asserting that you do not discriminate ("Equal Opportunity Employer"). However, the use of such a disclaimer carries no weight if you discriminate in hiring or if the ad itself is discriminatory. Ads which violate the Age Discrimination Act ("sharp recent grads," "recent high school grads") or which discriminate by sex ("Help Wanted—Male" or "Help Wanted—Female") are no less illegal simply because they have a disclaimer at the end.

Disparate Effect. Also called "adverse impact." If you have an employment policy that tends to allow more members of one group to qualify (for employment, training, promotion, etc.) than another, that policy may be violating the law because it is having an unequal (disparate) effect on different groups. It does not matter how neutral or unbiased the policy appears to be. It is the effect that counts. *Example:* Requiring applicants to have two "business" references might appear to be neutral, but in fact would tend to have an unfair effect on minorities living in inner city areas where unemployment is high and business references may be hard to come by.

Disparate Treatment. Enforcing rules, regulations, or other company policies differently for different groups. This kind of uneven treatment is a violation of Title VII. *Example:* A manager who closes one eye to tough job requirements for white males, allowing many to qualify, then applies the same job requirements rigidly for blacks or women so few of them qualify. Uneven enforcement of work, attendance, punctuality, safety, or other rules are also examples of disparate treatment, all of which violate Title VII.

EEOC Guidelines. Positions expressed by the EEOC that don't have the force of law but tend to be supported by the courts. These positions are outlined in various EEOC publications such as "Discrimination Because of Sex," "Discrimination Because of Religion," etc.

EEO-1 Report. An employer's annual report to the EEOC showing the percentage representation of women and minorities in each of the company's job categories. Companies with 100 or more employees file one, although federal contractors with 50 or more employees must file also.

English-Language Requirement. If you think a job requires an excellent command of English and want to rule out those with little or no English, be prepared to *prove* that the requirement is "essential" to the safe and efficient running of your operation. While the safety of co-workers or the public is a valid reason (a worker on an emergency repair crew needs to communicate for safety reasons), co-worker gripes or anxiety about customers' reaction to a foreign accent are not.

Final Findings. Also called "final determination." A state agency's decision on a discrimination charge as to whether or not it was valid. If the EEOC is considering investigating the charge itself, it will give "substantial weight" to the state agency's final findings before deciding whether or not to re-investigate.

Final Findings and Orders. An agreement between a company and state agency stating that the company will correct the discriminatory practice(s) that resulted in the complaint. The agreement may be enforced by the courts.

Handicapped Person. If your company does business with the federal government, you are required by the Rehabilitation Act of 1973 to take affirmative action for handicapped persons. In terms of the law, a handicapped person is anyone who has a physical or mental problem which "substantially limits" activities that may affect his or her employment. The definition also covers people who once had a physical or mental problem and have recovered, as well as those who only appear to have a limitation but do not. Since these individuals are discriminated against just as much as those who have cur-

Dealing with Day-to-Day Supervisory Problems 111

rent and real handicaps, they are covered by the law too.

Job Category. An overall grouping such as secretarial, administrative, production/maintenance. Called "Primary Occupational Activities" on some government reports.

Job Classification. Also called "Job Title." Refers to specific job level such as "Apprentice Welder," "Group Leader," "Clerk 4," etc.

Pre-Employment Contacts. Refers to help wanted ads, referrals, pre-employment applications, and other procedures for finding and recruiting job applicants. All of these procedures are fully covered by the EEO laws.

Probable (or Reasonable) Cause. In contrast to the "proof beyond a reasonable doubt" required in criminal cases, the EEOC and other government civil rights agencies need only find probable (or reasonable) cause to conclude that discrimination exists in an organization's employment practices.

"Red Circle" Rates. The courts have ruled that when minorities or women are shifted into jobs that were previously closed to them, jobs where people usually start at a lower wage than the minorities or women are receiving in their current work, their *current* wage rate should be kept ("red circled") until they reach an equivalent wage level in the new job. In other words, women and minorities are not supposed to take a paycut because they were prevented by discrimination from getting into certain kinds of work at an earlier time.

Remedial Action File. A list of qualified minority and female employees to be promoted at the next opportunity—usually into jobs from which they had formally been barred. Also refers to lists of qualified minority and female job applicants to be hired from outside the company the next time jobs open up.

Respondent. The company or organization named in a discrimination charge.

Retaliation. To take any action against someone for accusing you or your organization of discrimination, whether to your face or in a charge to a government agency, is a violation of Title VII. This also covers people who testify against you or in any way help others to file charges. It doesn't matter how accurate the charges are. Even people who make up shocking lies are protected. Retaliation may be anything from the cold shoulder to a change in job assignments to discharge or other discipline.

Reverse Discrimination. A non-legal term that refers to discrimination against white males. Usually phrased as "discrimination because of sex" (male) or "discrimination because of race" (white). An example of reverse discrimination might be firing a white male rather than offering him a lower paying job because you assumed that he would rather be unemployed than take a lower position.

Selection (or Hiring) Process. The steps involved in employment (or non-employment). Includes: Initial screening interview; filling out of application; tests for employment; background and/or reference checks; actual interview for employment; and decision whether or not to hire the individual.

706 Agency. When a discrimination charge is filed with the EEOC, the Commission is required by law to hand the charge over to a state or local government agency for investigation, which then has a minimum of 60 days to investigate. The agencies are nicknamed "706 agencies" because it is Section 706 of Title VII that requires the EEOC to defer charges to them.

Sexual Harassment. Refers to male managers demanding sexual favors from female subordinates in return for promotions, raises, or simply retaining their jobs. Courts are mixed on whether this is an EEO violation. Sometimes considered "disparate treatment" (see also) of women and therefore sex discrimination.

SSA. Abbreviation for Spanish-Surnamed American. Refers to people of Mexican, South American, Spanish origin, etc., who are covered by Title VII's prohibition against discrimination because of national origin.

Underutilization. Having a lower percentage of minorities or women in a particular "job category" than there is in your company's geographic hiring area.

Unlawful Employment Practice. Any policy or practice that discriminates and therefore violates one of the EEO laws. The *result* of the practice is what counts—not its *intent*.

We hope you found *The Affirmative Action Handbook* interesting and useful. We feel confident you will refer back to it often as supervisory problems arise.

Much of the material in this handbook has appeared in **THE EEO REVIEW,** a monthly newsletter which analyzes equal employment opportunity developments as they affect the manager and supervisor and assures a steady flow of vital information. Each issue contains cases and comments on current EEO problems. It also includes practical suggestions on legal rights, obligations, and pitfalls from attorneys specializing in EEO law.

THE EEO REVIEW is the *only* periodical available that is geared to the specific day-to-day EEO problems that confront employees in a supervisory capacity. As with *The Affirmative Action Handbook*, you will find **THE EEO REVIEW** down to earth, practical, and easy to read. The cost is minimal ($24/year for the first subscription and $18/year for each additional subscription); the benefits unlimited. Tear out and mail in the order form on the following page today.

ORDER FORM

EXECUTIVE ENTERPRISES
PUBLICATIONS CO., INC.
33 West 60th Street
New York, New York 10023

Please enter _____ subscription(s) to THE EEO REVIEW. Subscription rate is $24/year for the first subscription and $18/year for each additional subscription. Send the first monthly issue(s). If for any reason I am not totally satisfied, I may keep this issue—and get a full refund on the total price of my subscription(s).

NAME _____

TITLE _____

ORGANIZATION _____

ADDRESS _____

CITY _____ STATE _____ ZIP _____

PHONE NUMBER (Area Code) _____

SIGNATURE OR PURCHASE ORDER # _____

DOES NOT CIRCULATE